# Hebrew, Jewish, and Early Christian Studies

Hermit Kingdom Studies in
Christianity and Judaism 1

# Hebrew, Jewish, and Early Christian Studies

*Academic Essays*

Heerak Christian Kim

**The Hermit Kingdom Press**
Cheltenham ♦ Seoul ♦ Bangalore ♦ Cebu

**HEBREW, JEWISH, AND EARLY CHRISTIAN STUDIES: ACADEMIC ESSAYS**

Copyright © 2005 by Heerak Christian Kim

All rights reserved. No part of this book may be reproduced in any form or by any means, electronic or mechanical, including photocopying, recording, or by any information storage and retrieval system (including computer files in any form), without permission in writing from the publisher.

Hardcover: ISBN 1-59689-014-2
Paperback: ISBN 1-59689-015-0
Adobe E-Book: ISBN 1-59689-030-4

(USA) Library of Congress Control Number: 2005920778

*Write-To Address:*

The Hermit Kingdom Press
3741 Walnut Street, Suite 407
Philadelphia, PA 19104
United States of America

Info@TheHermitKingdomPress.com

\* \* \* \* \*

Hermit Kingdom
12 South Bridge, Suite 370
Edinburgh, EH1 1DD
Scotland

http://www.TheHermitKingdomPress.com

*For my father and mother*

# "I HAVE A DREAM...."

*Dr. Martin Luther King, Jr.*

# Contents

An Apology for God: Psalms of Solomon 11
and Its Jerusalem Tradition
🙵 1 ᘐ

An Agenda for Inclusive Ingathering:
A Case for a Christian Milieu
for the Gospel of John
🙵 30 ᘐ

Syntactical and Semantic
Consideration of בעוד
🙵 48 ᘐ

Ancient Inscriptions and
the Study of Biblical Hebrew
🙵 61 ᘐ

The Making of Theodor Herz,
the Father of the Jewish State of Israel
🙵 90 ᘐ

The Primacy of Immediate Small Group
Identity: A Criticism of Recent Nationalistic
Interpretations of the First Century
🙵 120 ᘐ

# Preface

This book contains six academic papers in the area of Hebrew linguistic/philological studies, Jewish historical studies, and early Christian/ New Testament studies, spanning over about a ten-year period.

My academic journey started in 1990, when I entered the Ph.D. program in the History Department of the University of California, Los Angles (UCLA) at the tender age of twenty. In the context of my doctoral research program at UCLA, I had the pleasure of going to Israel for the first time in 1993 with funding from the Goldsmith Foundation, the Hebrew University of Jerusalem, and the State of Israel.

1993 and Israel marked my entrance into professional academic life in earnest as the fruits of my research came to be presented at important academic conferences around the world. Since then I have never looked back.

I have spent over three years of intensive research in Israel and feel indebted to the academics there for my intellectual achievements. There are several professors at the Hebrew University of Jerusalem that I would like to thank particularly. Professor Avi Hurvitz guided my research and treated me like his own son. The fruit of research done in the field of Hebrew linguistics under Professor Hurvitz's aegis is clear in this volume.

I would also like to thank Professor Daniel Schwartz of the Department of Jewish History who showed me kindness and friendship. I had the pleasure of researching the concept of Jewish identity in the Second Temple period under his guidance. Fruits of research done with him were presented in academic conferences as well. And I hope to publish those papers in the near future.

I owe gratitude to Professor Michael Stone of the Department of Comparative Religion as well. Everyone who knows Professor Stone knows how likeable he is as a person. It took me by surprise at first because he is such an important scholar in the field. I particularly enjoyed seminars on apocrypha and pseudepigrapha held at his home. His children who had recently served in the Israeli military shared their experiences and helped me better understand Israeli culture. I thank the whole family for the kindness they have shown. Professor Stone has left an indelible mark on my approach to ancient texts and encouraged me to develop into a scholar in my own right. I will always be grateful.

I also learned from Profesor Moshe Greenberg (Aramaic Targums) and Professor Emmanuel

Tov (Dead Sea Scrolls) and I am deeply appreciative of all that I have learned from them.

While I was at the Hebrew University of Jerusalem, I had the pleasure of getting to know Israeli academics in less formal settings, such as over coffee or lunch; each conversation was a learning experience. Therefore, I would like to thank Professor Sarah Japhet, Professor Menachem Kister, Dr. Esther Chazon, Dr. David Satran, and Dr. Esti Eshel.

Of all the years I spent at the Hebrew University of Jerusalem, I had the pleasure of spending one year, 1995-96, as a Raoul Wallenberg Scholar. During that time, I had the opportunity to explore questions regarding democracy and human rights in the context of the program. I would like to thank two professors involved in that program: Professor Ehud Sprinzak and Professor Raymond Cohen, both of whom specialize on modern Israeli politics and society. Time spent in the program had an important impact on my personal development, which I hope will contribute to the betterment of the world and global peace.

Currently, I am in the process of completing my Ph.D. dissertation in Hebrew, Jewish, and Early Christian studies at the University of Cambridge under the guidance of a leading expert in the field. I would like to thank the Reverend

Professor William Horbury of Corpus Christi College, Cambridge, for his guidance and erudition. Much of my most recent creativity in the field is due to his excellent tutelage.

I am extremely grateful that I had the opportunities in my life to learn from some of the greatest minds in our time. But no amount of education and training will bear fruit without moral support.

I am truly fortunate in that I have the most supportive parents in the world. Mom and dad have always been there for me. Even when they were going through difficulties, they saved encouragement, support, and love for me. For their love, support, and prayers, I am eternally thankful. I would like to dedicate this book to them.

Heerak Christian Kim
Jesus College
Cambridge
United Kingdom
Dr. Martin Luther King, Jr.'s Birthday
2005

Hebrew, Jewish, and Early Christian Studies

# An Apology for God: Psalms of Solomon 11 and Its Jerusalem Tradition[*]

*Psalms of Solomon* 11 has often been examined as a primary source for understanding the concept of redemptive ingathering in the Second Temple period. Ryle and James [1] have particularly done wonderful work chronicling the celebratory tone of redemptive ingathering by sharing Old Testament texts upon which *Pss. Sol.* 11 is based. While affirming that *Pss. Sol.* 11 is useful for understanding the redemptive ingathering concept in the Second Temple period, I would like to argue that the primary purpose of *Pss. Sol.* 11 was an apology

---

[*] This paper was delivered in the Apocrypha and Pseudepigrapha section of the International Society of Biblical Literature conference in Groningen, the Netherlands, in July, 2004. This paper represents a part of my Ph.D. thesis research for the University of Cambridge. I would like to thank my Ph.D. supervisor, the Rev. Prof. William Horbury, who kindly guided read over the complete paper and offered helpful guidance. And I would like to thank Prof. Pierluigi Piovanelli, the chairperson of the Apocrypha and Pseudepigrapha section, who was particularly supportive.

[1] Herbert Edward Ryle and Montague Rhodes James, *Psalms of the Pharisees, Commonly Called the Psalms of Solomon* (Cambridge: At the University Press, 1891).

for God. The poet[2] intended to exonerate God from any guilt at the destruction of Israel and murder of Jews. The poet implicitly recognizes that Jews died for their wrongdoings. God merely acted as an objective judge to dispense justice and punishment.[3] In affirming God's role as a righteous judge, the poet aligns himself with the ethos of the Old Testament. *Psalms of Solomon* vividly indicates its dependence on the concept of God's righteous destruction

---

[2] I prefer the epithet "poet" to refer to the composer(s) of *Psalms of Solomon* because it best describes the genre of the work. S. E. Gillingham argues that a distinctive quality of Hebrew poetry, contra Greek or Latin poetry, was its emphasis on parallelism (S. E. Gillingham, *The Poems and Psalms of the Hebrew Bible* [Oxford: Oxford University Press, 1994], 73). Thus, Hebrew poetry was easily translatable to other languages and retained its fundamental characteristics in translation. Although James Kugel wants a broader understanding of parallelism, even he fundamentally acknowledges that a type (or types) of parallelism characterizes Hebrew poetry (James Kugel, *The Idea of Biblical Poetry* [New Haven: Yale University Press, 1981], 58). Using his understanding of Hebrew poetry, particularly of the Biblical psalms, Gillingham argues that *Psalms of Solomon* was originally written in Hebrew and represent later copies of earlier psalms (Gillingham, *The Poems and Psalms of the Hebrew Bible*, 263). On Hebrew poetry, also see T. H. Robinson's *The Poetry of the Old Testament* (London: Duckworth, 1947) and S. A. Geller's *Parellelism in Early Biblical Poetry* (Missoula: Scholars Press, 1979).
[3] Cf. *Pss. Sol.* 3:3; *Pss. Sol.* 10:5.

of Jews as the Old Testament sources for *Psalms of Solomon* indicate. The poet's apology for God is not only in his assertion for God's righteous execution of Jews, but also in his subsequent mercy and deliverance.[4] In fact, the poet assumes that the role of God as a righteous judge is understood and focuses on his role as a deliverer on a textual level. However, the poet shows himself to be an expert at using poetic devices of metaphor and parallel structure to remind the reader of God's mercy. Chief among them are the symbol of trumpet blowing and the use of the exodus structure to show God as righteous and free from blame.

First, I will turn my attention to the poet's implicit recognition of God as murdering Jews and destroying Israel. The Old Testament is replete with passages that

---

[4] The God of the exodus functions as the primary type for the God who ingathers. Thomas Dozeman explains in an enlightening way: "Priestly tridents fashion yet another view of divine power by merging both preexilic and deuteronomistic accounts of the exodus – a view that, in the end, must be interpreted as being a relational view of divine power. The predominant role of divine prediction provides a point of entry into the priestly view of divine power, and it illustrates how unilateral and relational views of divine power have been interwoven. The God of the exodus is certainly in control of all events for priestly tridents" (Thomas B. Dozeman, *God at War: Power in the Exodus Tradition* [New York: Oxford University Press, 1996], 130.

prophesy destruction of Israel (Hos 5; Amos 2:6-16; Isa 3; and Jer 6). In fact, it almost seems that Israel's prophets used the threat of destruction of Jerusalem to browbeat Jews into the worship of Yahweh. There are also many Old Testament passages indicating that God will kill Jews or will have Jews killed by the use of foreign powers (Isa 5:25-30; Isa 9:11-21; Isa 43:20-25; and Amos 4:10). The idea that God acted as a judge to deal out capital punishment to the Jews (Deut 4:3; Isa 10:22-23) is nothing new.[5] It may even be a truism to state that a Jew writing in a religiously Jewish setting took it for granted that God would punish Jews for transgressing the law.[6] Marinus de Jonge writes: "It is clear that the expectation of the realization of God's rule on earth

---

[5] Dozeman points out that Kabod Yahweh descending to judge in capital punishment (Num 16:19-50; Num 14:10, 21, 29-36) represents later priestly working over earlier deuteronomistic materials. For Dozeman the priestly reworking is in the substitution of Kabod Yahweh for the pillar of cloud appearing at the Tent of Meeting. Thus, Dozeman assumes that God's meting out capital punishment to Jews for violating God's law is consistent with the deuteronomistic (received) material (Dozeman, *God at War*, 125-126). This highlights that a large body of literature as well as philosophy existed for *Psalms of Solomon* to draw upon in formulating God's judgment.

[6] Marinus de Jonge, *Jewish Eschatology, Early Christian Christology and the Testament of the Twelve Patriarchs* (Leiden: Brill, 1991), 6.

is directly connected with the vision of the Torah of God, which was nurtured in the group of pious Jews in which the Psalms of Solomon originated."[7]

In the same way our poet takes for granted that God is a righteous judge (*Pss. Sol.* 8:9; cf. Isa 3:13-14) who has the implicit right to kill Jews in punishment either directly or by the use of foreign powers (*Pss. Sol.* 8:1-2, 15). The poet states this idea explicitly in *Pss. Sol.* 2.[8] Jews transgressed God's law, so God sent in foreign powers to kill them.[9] Experts on *Psalms of Solomon* often understood this to be the Romans and the account as describing specific events in Jewish history fresh in the readers' minds.[10] It is possible that the

---

[7] De Jonge, *Jewish Eschatology, Early Christian Christology and the Testament of Twelve Patriarchs*, 12.

[8] Marinus de Jonge assumes that *Pss. Sol.* 2 was written later than *Pss. Sol.* 8 (De Jonge, *Jewish Eschatology, Early Christian Christology and the Testament of the Twelve Patriarchs*, 7).

[9] Cf. Psalms of Solomon 17:10-18. For academic analysis of this concept, see Marinus de Jonge, "The Psalms of Solomon," in *Outside the Old Testament* (ed. Marinus de Jonge; Cambridge: Cambridge University Press, 1985), 160; also, R. B. Wright, "Psalms of Solomon," in *The Old Testament Pseudepigrapha Volume 2* (ed. James H. Charlesworth; London: Darton, Longman & Todd, 1985), 642.

[10] Robert R. Hann states: "In particular, the second, eighth, and seventeenth Psalms portray the reaction of their authors to the Roman occupation of Jerusalem in 63 BCE. These Jews understood for

event might describe Romans killing Jews. But it could just as well be Greeks killing Jews or Babylonians killing Jews.[11] For the purpose of the apology of the poet, whom God uses to kill Jews in divine retribution is irrelevant.

In the context of *Psalms of Solomon* as a whole, we can see that the explicit recognition of Jewish transgressions against God and the overt accounting of God's killing Jews by the use of foreign powers

---

righteousness on the part of the rulers and people of Israel (17:20)" (Robert R. Hann, *The Manuscript History of the Psalms of Solomon* [Chico: Scholars Press, 1982], 1).

[11] Marinus de Jonge makes a good point: "This leads us to the question of date. The PssSol do not describe historical events, but reflect them" (Marinus de Jonge, "The Psalms of Solomon," 161). The reflection is often universalizing in terms of larger principles – God is just, God punishes law breakers, God is merciful and redeems Jews. John I. Durham's comments about priestly source concerns are informative for our purposes. Durham argues that the overriding theme in Exodus 6:2-13 was the covenantal relationship between God and Israel. The focus between the two covenant parties made the identity of the third party inconsequential. Durham writes regarding the priestly redactor: "His interest was in a special relationship, as Israel's need in bondage, whether Egyptian or Assyrian or Babylonian or, for that matter, even Greek or Roman bondage, and as guaranteed as Israel's response to the active Presence of God could make it" (John I. Durham, *Exodus* [WBC 3; Waco: Word Books, 1987], 76). This characteristic also pervaded the thought-world of *Psalms of Solomon*.

particularly in the beginning parts of *Psalms of Solomon* set up the stage for *Pss. Sol.* 11. Certainly, in the final redacted form as we have *Psalms of Solomon* today, such an explicit recognition of God's right to kill Jews by using whichever foreign power he chooses functions to connect the Jews of the Late Second Temple period with the Old Testament concept of God's righteous retribution of Jews.[12] Although the final redacted form of *Psalms of Solomon* explicitly states God's right to carry out capital punishment against Jews for violating Torah, such overt statements were not needed. As indicated before, such an attitude was understood and fundamentally assumed.[13] Even if none of the earlier

---

[12] Momigliano argues that the making of the Torah in the Second Temple period caused Jews to abandon historiography (A. Momigliano, *The Classical Foundations of Modern Historiography* [Berkeley: University of California Press, 1990], 20). Dozeman agrees and states that the Torah went from being history to law. Writing history was, in fact, replaced by interpretation on the codified Torah (Dozeman, *God at War*, 177-178).

[13] The prevalence of such an attitude among the composers and their expected readers is found in the circle from which the composition originated. Scholarly consensus is for Pharisees (Ryle and James, *Psalms of the Pharisees, Commonly Called the Psalms of Solomon*, lix; A.-M. Dennis, *Introduction aux Pseudépigraphes grecs d'Ancient Testament* [Leiden: Brill, 1970], 64; Leonard Rost, *Einleitung in die alttestamentlichem Apokryphen und Pseudepigraphen* [Heidelberg: Quelle & Meyer,

portions of *Psalms of Solomon* survived and we only had *Pss. Sol.* 11, our starting point from a historical perspective would be that the poet assumes that God was righteous in using foreign powers to kill Jews.

The implicit assumption of this divine right is evident in *Pss. Sol.* 11. While Ryle and James see the trumpet blowing of *Pss. Sol.* 11 as indicating a type of Jubilee[14]

---

1971], 89-91). Some scholars have argued for its Essene origin due to its apocalyptic character (A. Dupont-Sommer, *The Essene Writings of Qumran* [Cleveland: Meridan, 1966], 296, 337; R. Wright, "The Psalms of Solomon, the Pharisees, and the Essenes," in *1972 Proceedings, International Organization for Septuagint and Cognate Studies* [ed. Robert A. Kraft; Missoula: Scholars Press, 1972], 146-147). Both of these communities assumed that God could and would punish for violation of the law and thus actively sought to observe the law. It should be noted, however, that Marinus de Jonge does not commit to either the Essene or the Pharisaic setting. De Jonge seems to be leaning in the direction of a Pharisaic circle, but he cautions: "A number of scholars have advocated Pharisaic origin, but we know too little of the tenets of the Pharisaic movement in the first century BC to be quite sure" (De Jonge, "The Psalms of Solomon," 160). De Jonge does not emphasize the religious intent of the Psalms of Solomon by asserting that it was written, or redacted, for use in a circle of pious men coming together in private houses and synagogues to study scriptures and to understand the signs of the times in a type of OT wisdom tradition (De Jonge, "The Psalms of Solomon," 160).

[14] Ryle and James, *Psalms of the Pharisees, Commonly Called the Psalms of Solomon*, 101. Also, see

as indicated in Joel 2, to limit it to that reference would be a mistake. Trumpet blowing to sound a jubilee, in fact, is not as widespread in the Old Testament as the trumpet blowing for war. References indicating trumpet blowing for war is found in vastly divergent texts within the Old Testament (Josh 6:2-21; 2 Chr 13:12; and Hos 5:8). Trumpet blowing in a war context could have served two purposes for the apologist for God.

The trumpet blowing was a reminder to the Jews of the war that God used to punish them (Jer 6:1-6). A good sense of this connotation can be seen in *Pss. Sol.* 1:2 where "the alarm of war" (κραυγὴ πολέμου) was heard as foreigners attacked.[15] More explicit reference to trumpet's warlike function can be found in *Pss. Sol.* 8:1. Like *Pss. Sol.* 1:2, "the sound of war" (φωνὴν πολέμου) is heard. This finds its poetic

---

J. Wellhausen, *Die Pharisäer und die Sadducäer: Eine Untersuchung zur inneren jüdischen Geschichte* (2nd edition; Hannover: Orient-Buchhandlung Heinz Lafaire, 1924), 155; S. Holm-Nielsen, "Psalemen Salomos" in *Jüdische Schriften aus hellenistisch-römischer Zeit, Band IV, Lieferung 2* (ed. W. G. Kümmel; Gütersloh: Mohn, 1977), 85-86; cf. E. E. Geiger, *Der Psalter Salomo's herausgeben und erklärt* (Augsburg: J. Wolffischen Buchhandlung, 1871), 138.

[15] Marinus de Jonge writes regarding sinners ('αμαρτωλοῖς): "clearly non-Jews" (Marinus de Jonge, "The Psalms of Solomon," p. 163).

parallel in "the sound of trumpet" (φωνὴν σάλπιγγος) in the same verse. "War" and "trumpet" are used as synonyms because the sounding of the trumpet was understood predominantly in its war context. Foreign powers came in, waged war, and killed Jews. As such, trumpet blowing in *Pss. Sol.* 11 reminds the reader of what happened before. God has righteously punished Jerusalem and Jews for their transgressions (*Pss. Sol.* 8:7, 15). It sets up the apologetic text nicely for the poet.

Secondly, trumpet blowing was a reminder to the Jewish readers that God wages war for them. The idea of "the Lord of the Hosts,"[16] or a militant Yahweh who wages war for Jews, is prominent in the Old Testament (Exod 15:3; Isa 42.13; 59:15-20).[17] The trumpet blowing indicated that

---

[16] Rikki E. Watts writes regarding Isaiah: "Whereas in chapters 1-39, the title יהוה צבאות with its warrior overtones primarily connoted judgment – as Yahweh had previously fought for Israel, now with 'outstretched arm' (5:25b; 9:11b, 16b, 20) he would fight against her (1:7-9, 24f.; 2:12; 3:1; 10:23 etc.) – in chapters 40-55, יהוה צבאות occurs primarily in salvation oracles which proclaim the NE (45:13; 47:4; 51:15; 54:5; cf. 13:1ff; 40:26)" (Rikki E. Watts, *Isaiah's New Exodus and Mark* [Tübingen: Mohr Siebeck, 1997], 141).

[17] God's warfare in the Bible is often genocidal. Gören Larsson points out that in the case of Moses turning Nile River to blood, it was a type of tit-for-tat. Egyptians tried to carry out genocides against the Israelites via the river (Exod 1:22), and it was used to

this militaristic God was fighting for them now and could affect a divine ingathering no matter how great their foe.[18] In both uses of trumpet blowing in a war context, the end

---

give a deadly blow that harbingered the final act of genocide (Gören Larsson, *Bound for Freedom: The Book of Exodus in Jewish and Christian Traditions* [Peabody: Hendrickson, 1999], 60). Josh 10:40 states that Israel's war program was one of genocide. James K. Hoffmeier argues that such a genocidal language was "hyperbolic" (James K. Hoffmeier, *Israel in Egypt: The Evidence for the Authenticity of the Exodus Tradition* [New York: Oxford University Press, 1997], 38). But if we take seriously Michael Fishbane's argument that "in the Hebrew Bible historical narrative is always narrative history, and so is necessarily mediated by language and its effects" (Michael Fishbane, "1 Samuel 3: Historical Narrative and Narrative Poetics," in *Literary Interpretation of Biblical Narratives, Volume 2* [ed. Kenneth R. R. Gros Louis; Nashville: Abingdon, 1982], 203), then the genocidal warfare program embraced in the narrative framework acquires the element of "fact," certainly in terms of Israelite *Weltanschauung*. Thomas B. Dozeman writes regarding God's genocidal warfare: "So important is this image of divine power that the annihilation of the enemy by Yahweh marks the moment of salvation for Israel and prompts its victory hymn of celebration in Exod 15:3, 'Yahweh is a warrior!'" (Thomas B. Dozeman, *God at War*, 3).

[18] The tenth prayer in the Eighteenth Benedictions ("The Amidah") proclaims trumpet-blowing for the ingathering of the exiles. The eleventh prayer shows that it is in the context of restoration from a state of judgment by God. Furthermore, the eleventh prayer specifically calls God King, thereby resounding his absolute rule and military role in victory.

result is to apologize for God and his righteousness – in his divinely just retribution for transgressions and in his mighty delivery and salvation.

Besides its military function, trumpet blowing in the Old Testament has important cultic implications. One prominent usage is the trumpet blowing to call people to proper cultic worship in Jerusalem (Isa 27:13). This idea seems congruent with the content of *Psalms of Solomon* as Jews are being ingathered to Jerusalem for cultic worship. Jews were not being ingathered to Jerusalem for social association or a non-religious assembly. Distinctively cultic tone is taken in *Pss. Sol.* 11 and it coincides with the ethos of the whole of *Psalms of Solomon*.

When we look at Joel 2, an Old Testament source for *Pss. Sol.* 11, we see that my arguments are supported. While it is true that as Ryle and James indicate, a type of Jubilee[19] is proclaimed in Joel 2, the concern of Joel 2 is more with proper cultic worship. Joel 2:15 specifically states: "Blow the trumpet in Zion, declare a holy fast, call a sacred assembly." Trumpet-

---

[19] George Wesley Buchanan argues that Israel's sin was perceived as incurring a debt. Thus, covenantal obligations required an exile to pay for debt on covenantal obligations. In the exile, Israel could look toward the Jubilee year when they would be released from their obligations (George Wesley Buchanan, *The Consequences of the Covenant* [Leiden: E. J. Brill, 1970], 6).

blowing was to announce proper cultic worship and assembly. It is important that Jews worship Yahweh in the way outlined in the law. Furthermore, Joel 2 indicates that trumpet blowing retains its military symbol explicitly and is thus consistent with the predominant use of trumpet blowing in the Old Testament. Joel 2:1 proclaims: "Blow the trumpet in Zion; sound the alarm on my holy hill. Let all who live in the land tremble, for the day of the LORD is coming." Joel, in fact, emphasizes both the killing of Jews by God in divine retribution (Joel 1) and the deliverance of Jews by God from larger enemies (Joel 3). The double-edged trumpet-blowing military symbol is stark in Joel. Ryle and James are right to refer to Joel 2 as a source for *Psalms of Solomon*. But it must be stressed that it is important to recognize trumpet blowing's more preponderant imageries that I have pointed out.

In fact, the two imageries reinforce each other. Trumpet blowing for proper cultic worship reminds the Jewish readers that if they do not gather for proper cultic worship, God will in essence blow the trumpet to have them killed by foreign powers.[20] On the other hand, if the Jews

---

[20] The idea that proper cultic participation is essential for God's protection was accepted as a narrative fact. Dozeman describes this context in light of the prevalent deuteronomistic framework: "The focus of

gather for proper cultic worship, God will blow the trumpet against Israel's enemies and defend them against their foes, no matter how great. George Wesley Buchanan writes regarding the import of proper cultic observance for Israel's military victory: "The God of armies fought the battles of Israel, but victory was not automatic. Sinlessness and faith were requirements for the people if they were to win."[21] In essence, therefore, trumpet blowing lands blame for Jewish death and destruction squarely on Jews and their transgressions (cf. Isa 3:8-9), thereby freeing God from any guilt. Thus, *Pss. Sol.* 11 implicitly recognizes God's right to annihilate Jews via foreign powers when Jews transgress against God.

Trumpet blowing in *Pss. Sol.* 11, grounded in the Old Testament narrative fact, therefore, functioned as a key apologetic tool for the poet. Furthermore, the poet functions as an apologist by explicitly emphasizing God's mercy. This is grounded in the idea that God can continue to kill Jews since Jews broke the covenant,

---

deuteronomistic interpretation, however, tended to be more exclusive in order to emphasize Israel's need to participate in cultic action in order to avoid the plague of death" (Dozeman, *God at War*, 129). In essence, God's judgment of Israelite's enemies will not exclude Israelites who do not offer proper cultic worship.

[21] Buchanan, *The Consequences of the Covenant*, 6.

but God extends mercy and delivers Jews in divine ingathering. In fact, the poet asserts a type of "God is more righteous than he ought to be" thesis in his apology for God. Thus, God's mercy in divine ingathering takes center stage in *Pss. Sol.* 11 to show God's infinite righteousness and freedom from guilt.

And God's great mercy is highlighted in *Pss. Sol.* 11 in an elaborate literary structure. To make his apology more effective, the poet utilizes the literary structure of the exodus to accomplish his argument for God's mercy.[22] As a literary motif, the exodus served as a reminder and symbol of God's faithfulness to his covenant.[23] It chronicled for the Jews a reality of the deliverance by God whereby God vanquished an enemy far greater than they and brought the Jews safely into the promised land. It was a clear evidence for God's mercy in spite of their faithlessness to

---

[22] Dozeman argues that the Book of Exodus represents exilic transformation into salvation history of preexilic liturgy celebrating the holy war victories of Yahweh at the sea (Dozeman, *God at War*, p. 4). In the process of this literary transformation, exodus became an archetype of God's salvation patterns for later generations.

[23] In fact, Roland de Vaux agues that the exodus 'was to remain in the mind of the people of Israel as their most important historical and religious memory' (Roland de Vaux, *The Early History of Israel: To the Exodus and Covenant of Sinai* [trans. David Smith; London: Darton, Longman & Todd, 1978], 320).

the covenant. Furthermore, the exodus served as an ideal model for religious leaders and those who wanted to centralize Jewish religion because of the explicitly stated purpose that the deliverance was for proper cultic worship in Jerusalem.

The poet utilizes the literary structure of the exodus[24] in his own way to meet the needs of his audience and his purpose of apologetics. Like the exodus account, *Pss. Sol.* 11 emphasizes God's miraculous and powerful involvement in the delivery process.[25] God's miracles were important to affirm God's mighty power. Just as in the exodus account, when God used miracles to deliver Israelites, God is portrayed in *Pss. Sol.* 11 as using his

---

[24] John I. Durham argues that the Book of Exodus is the first book of the Bible with a "one-track" focus (Durham, *Exodus*, xix). Durham writes: "God is first of all a God at hand, a God with his people, a God who rescues, protects, guides, provides for, forgives, and disciplines the people who call him *their* God and who call themselves *his* people" (Durham, *Exodus*, xxiii). Thus, exodus becomes a type of *Urtext* and takes on a proto-theme upon which later biblical and intertestamental religious literature is based.

[25] Roland de Vaux writes: "The faith of Israel was based on the interventions that the people of God made in their history and their cult was the expression of that faith and the commemoration of that history of their salvation" (De Vaux, *The Early History of Israel: To the Exodus and Covenant of Sinai*, 324).

miracles to deliver. Particularly, nature manipulation [26] is emphasized. As God brought gnats into the city to destroy and hail from sky to kill Israelites' enemies, God in *Pss. Sol.* 11 made the hills straight and trees to shade in the wilderness.

Besides the emphasis on God's miraculous delivery that attests to his mercy, there is a shared emphasis on the ingathering, also a sign of God's mercy. In the exodus account, God is portrayed as guiding Israelites out of Egypt through the wilderness and into the promised land. God is actually involved as indicated by the presence of God going before the Israelites (Exod 13:21; 14:19). A pillar of cloud by day or a pillar of fire by night guided the Israelites (Num 14:14).[27] God's merciful

---

[26] Nature manipulation in God's deliverance is an important exodus idea that is widely reiterated in the Old Testament; for example, in Isa 40:4 and Isa 42:15.

[27] God's presence is represented in the theophanic cloud in the exodus (Exod 33:11; Num 12:5; Deut 31:15; Neh 9:12, 19). Medieval Judaism became increasingly uncomfortable with a direct presence of God. Writing in the twelfth century, Rabbi Samuel ben Meir (Rashbam) stated in his commentary on Exod 13:21 and Exod 14:19 that an angel moved the pillar of cloud. Rashbam opposed any theophany of God in a cloud. Even earlier Rabbinic sources took issue with a direct theophanic presence in a cloud. Talmudic and midrashic sources describe God as moving the clouds, rather than being present actively in a physical manifestation (*Qidd.* 32a, *B. Qam.* 92b,

delivery, therefore, is portrayed as one of active involvement.

Likewise, in *Pss. Sol.* 11, God's merciful deliverance in divine ingathering is portrayed as one of active involvement. In fact, God is portrayed as directly involved without a mediating agent. In the context of *Pss. Sol.* 11, there isn't a messianic agent; it is God himself who will ingather the Jews. The emphatic pointing to God as the one who redeems indicates using the exodus material in a more intensely cultic form. The poet was writing after the impact of radical monotheism and exhibit influences from that school of thought. It is true that other parts of *Psalms of Solomon*, such as chapters 17 and 18, seem to indicate a more messianic salvation. Specifically, *Pss. Sol.* 17:32 has "Christ the Lord" (χριστὸς κύριος),[28] which is attested in Luke 2:11

---

*'Abod. Zar.* 11a and *Mekilta*). In this sense, Rabbinic sources exhibit greater influence from later Second Temple texts emphasizing God's use of mediating, or messianic agent. Direct acting of God as presented in *Pss. Sol.* 11 represents greater continuity with radical monotheism that came before it rather than the later Second Temple trend toward a mediating agent. In this regard, the Septuagint is faithful to the Hebrew text. The Septuagint has God ('ο θεός) leading ('ηγεῖτο) the Israelites for Exodus 13:21. For Exod 14:19, the Septuagint is faithful to the Hebrew text in not describing the angel as punishing the theophanic cloud.

[28] J. Schüpphaus preferred to read this as χριστὸς κυρίου, positing a transmission error (J. Schüpphaus,

(σωτὴρ 'ὅς ἐστιν χριστὸς κύριος). I would argue that these are later works added in the

---

*Die Psalmen Salomos* [Leiden: Brill, 1977], 71; cf. J. Wellhausen, *Die Pharisäer und die Sadducäer* 132). There is an assumption that the original composition was in Hebrew and that the Old Testament precedent was the Old Testament royal title of "the Lord's anointed" (משיח יהוה). J. Viteau explores the possibility of the genitive (κυρίου) read as a nominative due to a Christian theological influence (J. Viteau, *Les Psaumes de Salomon* [Paris: Letouzey et Ané, 1911], 361-2). It is more likely, however, that this phrase in the nominative state in the manuscript (all but two) indicates an interpolation at a later stage of textual redaction. I would argue that *Pss. Sol.* 17 and 18 were later than other parts of *Psalms of Solomon*, certainly *Pss. Sol.* 11. *Psalms of Solomon* 17 (and 18) could have been originally a Jewish text that experienced a Christian interpolation (or influence). It is also possible that *Pss. Sol.* 17 and 18 were Christian texts, perhaps written by a Jewish Christian. Furthermore, although the scholarly assumption is that the original was in Hebrew, it would be helpful to explore the possibility of a combination of Hebrew and Greek texts in the compositional process (or even an original Greek composition). On the possibility of a Greek original, see A. Hilgenfeld, "Die Psalmen Salomos und die Himmelfahrt des Moses, griechisch hergestellt und erklärt," ZWT 11 (1868): 133-68. The fact that First Baruch, which the accepted academic consensus assumes was an original Greek composition, quotes *Psalms of Solomon* (Bar 5:5-8; *Pss. Sol.* 11:2-5) encourages a more serious examination of a possible Greek original for *Psalms of Solomon*. This does not negate the possibility that the poet(s) composed in a distinctively Hebrew-poetry style. A style of writing can easily transcend the language barrier, particularly when that style is content-based (parallelism).

redaction process.[29] The original composer of *Pss. Sol.* 11 held more to radical monotheism, even shying away from messianic agents. It is possible that the composer was disillusioned by the shenanigans of the high priesthood. Whatever may have been the motivation, the psalmist privileging God's direct involvement is in line with Exodus' literary

---

[29] For instance, the term "anointed of the Lord" is found in *Pss. Sol.* 17:32. Marinus de Jonge notes that this term was "a designation used for the king in the Old Testament and especially in the royal Psalms. It is striking that this expression is never used in the Old Testament for a king or any other person to appear in the future. This usage is found for the first time in the intertestamental period, and the Psalms of Solomon 17 is one of the first passages in which this term is used in this way" (De Jonge, *Jewish Eschatology, Early Christian Christology and the Testament of the Twelve Patriarch*, 10). De Jonge's note on the deviation from the Old Testament is significant. I would argue that *Pss. Sol.* 11 was more faithful to the received tradition and was a separate composition from *Pss. Sol.* 17-18, which provided a messianic figure with a messianic title. Even de Jonge notes: "It is important to notice that this figure of a royal Anointed of the Lord, is mentioned only in Psalms 17 and Psalms 18. In Psalms 11 it is God Himself who will bring about the release and the return of the dispersed Jews to Israel. Also in other psalms, which relate a future intervention of God (Ps 7:10; 8:27-31; 10:5-8; 12:6; cf. 9:8-11; 14:9, 10; 15:12, 13) no Anointed is mentioned" (De Jonge, *Jewish Eschatology, Early Christian Christology and the Testament of the Twelve Patriarchs*, 11).

structure pointing to God's mercy, proven by his directly involved deliverance.

Another exodus element is poignantly present in *Pss. Sol.* 11; namely, the goal of divine ingathering. Exodus is clear that the reason for divine ingathering was for proper cultic worship. "Let my people go so that they may worship me" (Exod 8:1, 20; 9:1, 13; 10:3). Terence E. Fretheim writes: "Worship is a central theme of Exodus, the overall movement of the book is from slavery to worship. The concern for the proper worship of Yahweh is also evident throughout the book, seen both in specific content and in the fact that liturgical usage of this material has shaped the literature."[30] This, in fact, was an evidence of God's mercy. Israelites' ancestors left the promised land, thereby breaking God's covenant with Abraham. God had every right to allow Israelites to rot in servitude. However, God gave Israelites another chance at realizing their covenant obligations (Exod 24:1-11; Exod 34:10).[31] Thus, God took pains to deliver the Israelites so that they could worship properly on the covenantal ground.

---

[30] Terence E. Fretheim, *Exodus* (Louiville: John Knox Press, 1991), 20.

[31] Fretheim notes that the covenant of Sinai should be seen in the context of an existent covenant; namely, the Abrahamic covenant (Fretheim, *Exodus*, 257-258).

This merciful, redemptive act of God, emphasized in the exodus, is stressed in *Pss. Sol.* 11. Jews in the Diaspora who have violated the covenant and the law of God, were given a chance again to engage in proper cultic worship of God in Jerusalem. The idea of God's mercy in spite of Jewish violation of the covenant is highlighted in the concept of "forever" in *Pss. Sol.* 11. The Hebrew equivalent עולם ("forever") invokes the idea of ברית עולם ("everlasting covenant"). Roland de Vaux stresses God's covenantal mercy in these terms:

> What he does is to insist on the pre-eminence of the covenant, $b^e rîth$ *'ôlām*, a 'covenant in perpetuity' (Gen 17:7, 13, 19), not a bilateral pact, but a gracious initiative on God's part, a personal commitment in which he binds himself to a promise.... When the descendants of Abraham, Isaac and Jacob became a people, they were integrated, as a people, into the covenant made with their fathers. The reference to the covenant concluded on Mount Sinai at the end of the Law of Holiness (Lev 26:45) is preceded by a reminder of the

covenant with Abraham (Lev 26:42).[32]

I agree with de Vaux that the Sinai covenant and the Abrahamic covenant show the idea of the grace of God in ברית עולם. But I would argue that God's mercy was in the very fact that he chose to keep the covenant while Israel broke their part since ברית עולם was a contract mutually binding the two parties in perpetuity, rather than merely binding God alone. The covenant idea in exodus (also, embodying the idea of the Abrahamic covenant), thus, came to function as a connecting symbol for God's mercy in later Jewish literature, such as *Psalms of Solomon*. Like the exodus, *Pss. Sol.* 11 indicates that the Jews were being ingathered in Jerusalem for proper cultic worship. "Holy robe" (*Pss. Sol.* 11:8) is a language indicating priestly vestments described in detail in Exod 39. It is a symbol and a metaphor for proper cultic worship. And just as in exodus, this act of God represented mercy and covenant renewal in spite of Israel's faithlessness. God was giving them another chance.

  The literary structure of *Pss. Sol.* 11 certainly draws on the exodus material. The poet strategically highlights the mercy of God in his miraculous deliverance in ingathering the Jews to Jerusalem even

---

[32] De Vaux, *The Early History of Israel*, 397.

though Jews were deserving of divine retribution for their transgressions. But the poet made it clear that God had the right to kill Jews, even by using foreign armies, in righteous punishment. With the collective memory of enemy armies, blowing trumpet and slaughtering Jews, the poet was particularly interested in exonerating God from blame and placing the blame squarely on Jews. With Old Testament sources and narrative facts as implicitly accepted facts, the poet of *Pss. Sol.* 11 adeptly arranged his poem as an apologetic masterpiece to declare God as righteous and a merciful judge, who has done nothing wrong.

# Bibliography

Buchanan, George Wesley. *The Consequences of the Covenant*. Leiden: Brill, 1970.

De Jonge, Marinus. *Jewish Eschatology, Early Christian Christology and the Testament of the Twelve Patriarchs*. Leiden: Brill, 1991.

De Jonge, Marinus. "The Psalms of Solomon." Pages 159-177 in *Outside the Old Testament*. Edited by Marinus de Jonge. Cambridge: Cambridge University Press, 1985.

De Vaux, Roland. *The Early History of Israel: To the Exodus and Covenant of Sinai*. Translated by David Smith. London: Darton, Longman & Todd, 1978.

Dennis, A.-M. *Introduction aux Pseudépigraphes grecs d'Ancient Testament*. Leiden: Brill, 1970.

Dozeman, Thomas B. *God at War: Power in the Exodus Tradition*. New York: Oxford University Press, 1996.

Dupont-Sommer, A. *The Essene Writings of Qumran*. Cleveland: Meridan, 1966.

Durham, John I. *Exodus*. Word Biblical Commentary 3. Waco: Word Books, 1987.

Fishbane, Michael. "I Samuel 3: Historical Narrative and Narrative Poetics." Pages 191-203 in *Literary Interpretations of Biblical Narratives, Volume 2*. Edited by Kenneth R. R. Gros Louis. Nashville: Abingdon, 1982.

Fretheim, Terence E. *Exodus*. Louisville: John Knox Press, 1991.

Geiger, E. E. *Der Psalter Salomo's herausgegeben und erklärt*. Augsburg: J. Wolffischen Buchhandlung, 1871.

Geller, S. A. *Parallelism in Early Biblical Poetry*. Missoula: Scholars Press, 1979.

Gillingham, S. E. *The Poems and Psalms of the Hebrew Bible*. Oxford: Oxford University Press, 1994.

Hann, Robert R. *The Manuscript History of the Psalms of Solomon*. Chico: Scholars Press, 1982.

Hilgenfeld, A. "Die Psalmen Salomos und die Hmmelfahrt des Moses, griechisch hergestellt und erklärt." *Zeitschrift für wissenschaftliche Theologie* 11 (1868): 133-68.

Hoffmeier, James K. *Israel in Egypt: The Evidence for the Authenticity of the Exodus Tradition*. New York: Oxford University Press, 1997.

Holm-Nielsen, S. "Psalmen Salomos." Pages 51-112 in *Jüdische Schriften aus hellenistisch-römischer Zeit, Band IV, Lieferung 2*. Edited by W. G. Kümmel. Gütersloh: Mohn, 1977.

Kugel, James. *The Idea of Biblical Poetry*. New Haven: Yale University Press, 1981.

Larsson, Gören. *Bound for Freedom: The Book of Exodus in Jewish and Christian Traditions*. Peabody: Hendrickson, 1999.

Momigliano, A. *The Classical Foundations of Modern Historiography*. Berkeley: University of California Press, 1990.

Robinson, T. H. *The Poetry of the Old Testament*. London: Duckworth, 1947.

Rost, Leonard. *Einleitung in die alttestamentlichem Apokryphen und Pseudepi-*

*graphen.* Heidelberg: Quelle & Meyer, 1971.

Ryle, Herbert Edward, and Montague Rhodes James. *Psalms of the Pharisees, Commonly Called the Psalms of Solomon.* Cambridge: At the University Press, 1891.

Schüpphaus, J. *Die Psalmen Salomos.* Leiden: Brill, 1977.

Viteau, J. *Les Psaumes de Salomon.* Paris: Letouzey & Ané, 1991.

Watts, Rikki E. *Isaiah's New Exodus and Mark.* Tübingen: Mohr Siebeck, 1997.

Wellhausen, J. *Die Pharisäer und die Sadducäer: Eine Untersuchung zur inneren jüdischen Geschichte.* 2$^{nd}$ edition. Hannover: Orient-Buchhandlung Heinz Lafaire, 1924.

Wright, R. "The Psalms of Solomon, the Pharisees, and the Essenes" Pages 136-154 in *1972 Proceedings, International Organization for Septuagint and Cognate Studies.* Edited by Robert A. Kraft. Missoula: Scholars Press, 1972.

Wright, R. B. "Psalms of Solomon." Pages 639-670 in *The Old Testament Pseude-*

*pigrapha Volume 2*. Edited by James H. Charlesworth. London: Darton, Longman & Todd, 1985.

## An Agenda for Inclusive Ingathering: A Case for a Christian Milieu for the Gospel of John[*]

The ingathering concept in the Gospel of John is a window into the character of the Johannine community and its emphasis on radically inclusive mission. In order to emphasize that Gentiles are included in the "children of God," the Johannine literature radically reinterprets traditional understanding of redemptive ingathering extant in the late Second Temple period. In the apologetic process, the Gospel writer employs anti-Jewish polemic of exclusivity as his literary tool, and this is clearly evident (and forms an essential part) of the restructuring of the traditional ingathering formula. It is crucial, however, to understand the background out of which this reconstruction played a role as the staring point and provide a more lucid understanding of the character and theology of the Johannine community. In this paper, I will argue that it is worth-

---

[*] This paper was delivered at the British New Testament Conference in Birmingham, UK, in September, 2003. This is a part of the research for the Ph.D. dissertation at the University of Cambridge, and I would like to thank my Ph.D. supervisor, Rev. Prof. William Horbury for reading the complete paper and offering many helpful suggestions.

while to revisit C. H. Dodd and Rudolf Bultmann's understanding of the socio-theological milieu out of which the Gospel of John arose. I will posit that it is helpful to incorporate common element in both writers claiming or implying a type of Christian milieu. Based on this construction of the socio-theological milieu, I will explain the distinctive Christian apologetic character of the Gospel of John particularly as relating to ingathering. In the process, I will particularly examine the pericope in the Gospel of John 11:45-54 relating to ingathering as a direct evidence for my claims.

I would like first to posit that it is helpful to understand the existence of a Christian milieu. In arguing for a Christian milieu, I am positing a self-conscious and defined awareness of being Christian, marked by distinctively Christian claims. In negative terms, a Christian milieu militates against understanding Gospel of John as arising out of a Jewish or Hellenistic milieu with negligible Christian self-awareness. In emphasizing the Christian milieu for understanding Johannine community and its theology (including ingathering), I find Rudolf Bultmann and C. H. Dodd's works particularly helpful. I believe that their ideas must be revisited and their understanding (whether consciously stated or implicitly implied) of a Christian milieu emphasized.

Recently, there has been some tendency for Bultmann's central ideas on John to move into the background with exceptions, such as exemplified in the work of John Ashton.[1] This is unfortunate because I believe that he has important insight that can advance better understanding of John. Rudolf Bultmann understands the Gospel of John as a product of Gnostic influences in a Semitic setting. Bultmann writes: "On the one hand John manifests close contacts with the Gnostic conception of the world. The source of the discourses, which John takes over or to which he alludes, is Gnostic in outlook."[2] Bultmann particularly points to cosmic dualism in the Gospel of John as indicative of Gnostic quality. However, Bultmann is careful to assert that Gnosticism was an outside influence on Christianity. Bultmann writes: "It [Gnosticism] has its roots in a dualistic redemption-religion which invaded Hellenism from the orient."[3] Fundamentally, Christian Gnosticism is different from that which influenced it. Bultmann writes: "Unlike heathen Gnosticism, Christian Gnosticism naturally could

---

[1] John Ashton, *Understanding the Fourth Gospel* (Oxford: Clarendon Press, 1991) 113.
[2] Rudolf Bultmann, *The Gospel of John: A Commentary*, trans. G. R. Beasley-Murray (Oxford: Basil Blackwell, 1971) 8.
[3] Rudolf Bultmann, *Theology of the New Testament (Vol. 1)*, trans. Kendrick Grobel (London: SCM Press Ltd., 1952) 109.

not give up all connection with the historical person Jesus and thus transplant the occurrence of salvation into a mystic past."[4] The Gospel of John, tending toward Christian Gnosticism, is no different; it maintains the distinctive quality that makes it Christian. But Bultmann argues that focus on Jesus is particularly pronounced in the Gospel of John. Bultmann writes: "The Gospel of John fundamentally contains but a single theme: the Person of Jesus. The entire Gospel is concerned with the fact of his presence, the nature of his claim, whence he comes and wither he goes, and how men relate themselves to him."[5] And it is this theological focus that sets the Johannine Gospel apart from the Synoptic Gospels. Bultmann writes: "The narrative material, especially the passion story and the accounts of John the Baptist, has the closest contact of all with the corresponding elements in the Synoptic tradition. But even in these respects the author has more or less strongly interposed, transformed and completed them in accordance with his theological views."[6] For Bultmann, it is significant that the Gospel of John arose in an oriental setting with source influences from Gnosticism, but

---

[4] Rudolf Bultmann, *Theology of the New Testament (Vol. 2)*, trans. Kendrick Grobel (London: SCM Press, 1955) 126.
[5] Bultmann (1971) 5.
[6] Bultmann (1971) 4.

the overarching characteristic is Johannine theology, which shaped the Gospel of John.

The situation of composition is not very different from Paul's writings. Bultmann argues that Paul's writings also arose in an oriental setting with strong Gnostic influences present in Hellenistic Christianity. The probable influence was mediated through Hellenistic Judaism, according to Bultmann. Bultmann writes:

> It is clear: Hellenistic Christianity is in the maelstrom of the syncretic process; genuinely Christian element is wrestling with other elements; 'orthodox' does not exist at this early period but is still to develop. At first, Gnosticism probably penetrated into the Christian congregations mostly through the medium of a Hellenistic Judaism that was itself in the grips of syncretism. The Gnostic Spirit-enthusiasts whom Paul opposes at Corinth are of Jewish origin (II Cor. 11:22).[7]

Thus, Paul, working in the framework of Hellenistic Christianity heavily influenced

---
[7] Bultmann (1952) 171.

by Gnosticism, opposes a brand of Gnosticism that does not have the distinctively Christian element, namely Christ.

This portrayal of Paul by Bultmann is reminiscent of his portrayal of John. Both groups of writing arose in an oriental setting with heavy influences of Gnosticism. Bultmann writes: *"The descent and re-ascent of the Redeemer* is the subject of Eph. 4:8-10."[8] This point of Bultmann's highlights the similarity with John. The idea of descent and ascent is integral to the Gospel of John.

But for Bultmann, it is the similarity that highlights the difference between John and Paul. Bultmann writes: "Since there is such contact with common Christian terminology in both John and Paul, it is all the more significant that *the specifically Pauline terminology is missing in John.*"[9] Bultmann is emphatic about the lack of connection between Paul and John. Bultmann writes: "Clearly, then, John is not of the Pauline school and is not influenced by Paul; he is, instead, a figure with his own originality and stands in an atmosphere of theological thinking different from that of Paul."[10] For Bultmann, particularly different is the language of salvation. John does not use "righteousness of God" (δικαιοσυνη θεου)

---

[8] Bultmann (1952) 175.
[9] Bultmann (1955) 7.
[10] Bultmann (1955) 9.

to indicate salvation itself.[11] But it is not merely divergence in terminology that sets John apart. In fact, Bultmann argues that theological understanding of salvation is different in John. Bultmann states that in the Gospel of John it is not only his death that served atonement for sin; rather, Jesus' sacrifice includes his whole ministry as well.[12]

Although Bultmann works hard to separate John from Paul, questions rise as to the legitimacy of his arguments. Bultmann's argument is dependent on the dating schema he proposes and on the basis of the power of the redactional process. Bultmann argues that the composition of the Gospel of John was quite late; in fact, he asserts that it was composed well after the destruction of Jerusalem in 70 AD. Bultmann writes: "So far as the situation of the Church is reflected in the Gospel of John, its problem is the conflict with Judaism, and its theme is faith in Jesus as the Son of God. The Christian congregation is already excluded from the synagogue association (9:22; 16:1-3)...."[13]

Historical development along with specifically Joannine theological concerns resulted in reshaping of the sources. Thus, the radical conflict with Judaism and violent criticism of Jews must be seen as the

---

[11] Bultmann (1955) 8.
[12] Bultmann (1955) 53-54.
[13] Bultmann (1955) 5.

product of the redaction. Early Christian community was experiencing antagonism from Judaism, and the Gospel of John provides a picture of this struggle. Even accounts of Jews attempting to stone Jesus and Jesus' polemic against Jews are to be understood as being from the author of the Gospel of John.

Implicitly, however, Bultmann recognizes that there was a type of Christian milieu from which the author of the Gospel of John operated. The Gospel of John arose out of already established Christian community with a history based on established Christian traditions and common experiences. Thus, in essence, the redaction stage provided a reshaping of materials that were already distinct from Judaism of the time. In this sense, Bultmann's argument that it is important to see Christianity as distinctive from Judaism and Paganism is helpful. In fact, this was the self-perception of the early Christians, and this separation is quite early in Christian self-consciousness. And it was this Christian self-consciousness which is a fundamental evidence for the Christian milieu. In this light, while identifying differences, it might be helpful to tone down the over-emphasis on the distinctiveness of the Gospel of John vis-à-vis other Christian communities and literary traditions within early Christianity.

C. H. Dodd's explication of the Gospel of John and its composition process involves identifying socio-literary influences and environment. In his monograph, *The Interpretation of the Fourth Gospel*, Dodd considers literary trends with which the Gospel of John shares similar traits. Dodd discusses similarities found in the Hermetic literature, Hellenistic Judaism, Rabbinic Judaism, Gnosticism, and Mandaism. Although Dodd readily recognizes similarities, he is less eager to identify these literary trends as direct influences on the Gospel of John. Dodd's cautious attitude is reflected in his comment about Hermetic literature. Dodd writes: "It seems clear that as a whole they represent a type of religious thought akin to one side of Johannine thought, without any substantial borrowing on the one part or the other. It is when we have done justice to this kinship that we are likely to recognize the full significance of those elements in Johannine thought which are in striking contrast to *Hermetica*, and in which we must seek the distinctively Christian teaching of the Fourth Gospel."[14] In fact, this cautious attitude to similarities between John and the Hermetic literature guides Dodd's examination of other literary trends.

---

[14] C. H. Dodd, *The Interpretation of the Fourth Gospel* (Cambridge: At the University Press, 1958) 53.

The caution can be attributed to Dodd's emphasis that the Gospel of John, like other Christian texts, must be seen as originating from a common Christian milieu. Dodd writes regarding the Gospel of John: "It is clear, to begin with, that the gospel has behind it the common Christianity of the early period, and that readers who shared the life and thought of the Church would find here much that was familiar...."[15] In fact, Dodd argues that early Christians showed the common experience of a living community focusing on the words of Jesus. The dynamic nature of primitive Christian experience, in effect, was at the heart of the Christian milieu, which influenced Christian writings. Dodd writes:

> The early Church was not such a bookish community as it has been represented. It did its business in the world primarily through the medium of the living voice, in worship, teaching and missionary preaching, and out of these three forms of activity – liturgy, *didache*, *kerygma* – a tradition was built up, and this tradition lies behind all literary production of the

---

[15] Dodd (1958) 6.

early period, including our written gospels.[16]

Dodd is more explicit than Bultmann in pointing to a common Christian milieu. Furthermore, Dodd is willing to allow greater impact of common Christian influence than Bultmann, although Bultmann operates from an implicit acknowledgement of a Christian milieu that influenced Christian writings.

It is understandable why Dodd emphasizes the Christian milieu and its significant influence. Essential to Dodd's approach to the New Testament is the idea that kerygma, or the "spoken Gospel," forms the core of the "written Gospel." Dodd, in essence, emphasizes the original teaching of Jesus as being traceable in the written Gospel.[17] In this regard, Dodd stands opposed to the demythologization hypothesis of Bultmann, which puts greater emphasis on redaction and takes a pessimistic view of the preservation of the kerygma. Dodd casts doubt on the academic tradition which Bultmann pushed. Dodd writes: "The 'quest of the historical Jesus,' which stimulated the critical study of the New Testament in the nineteenth century, is by

---

[16] C. H. Dodd, *Historical Tradition in the Fourth Gospel* (Cambridge: At the University Press, 1963) 8.

[17] Dodd (1963) 22.

some of the most influential theologians of our time no longer believed to be a profitable, or indeed a feasible, enterprise."[18] Dodd argues that this approach is not constructive because it misunderstands the nature of the early Christian text. Dodd writes: "A study of the theological symbolism and typology embodied in the gospels will (it is urged) bring us further in understanding them than any attempt to establish a residuum of factual record. In any case they were written (in the current cliché) 'from faith to faith.' To seek in them sources of historical information is to misunderstand their character and the intention of their authors."[19]

Although Dodd disagrees with Bultmann in regards to the degree of effectiveness of kerygmatic transmission, he agrees with Bultmann in emphasizing distinctiveness of the Gospel of John. Dodd states emphatically: "There is no book, either in the New Testament or outside it, which is really *like* the Fourth Gospel."[20] And like Bultmann, Dodd is careful to assert the independence of the Gospel of John from Pauline influence. Dodd writes: "That the evangelist has not escaped the powerful influence of the first great Christian theologian whose works are extant, is probable

---

[18] Dodd (1963) 1.
[19] Dodd (1963) 1.
[20] Dodd (1958) 6.

enough. But the actual range of Pauline influence upon Johannine thought has been exaggerated. Those who tie John down too closely to the Pauline tradition are inclined to undervalue his distinctive contribution to the religion and theology of early Christianity."[21] It is important, however, to note that Dodd believes that the common Christian milieu influenced both John and Paul.

I would posit that it is important to emphasize that a Christian milieu was the causative environment out of which the Gospel of John arose. This predominantly Christian environment sought to emphasize Christian distinctives surrounding the person and work of Jesus of Nazareth. Negatively, this Christian milieu militated against a Jewish understanding of the Old Testament on a conscious and subconscious levels. Thus, Barnabas Lindars focuses on the apologetic tendency of Johannine theology.[22] Raymond Brown emphasizes that conflict with Pharisaic Judaism is crucial for understanding the Gospel.[23] In other words, both the positive identification and negative identification in the self-definition of

---

[21] Dodd (1958) 5.
[22] Barnabas Lindars, *New Testament Apologetic: The Doctrinal Significance of the Old Testament Quotations* (London: SCM Press Ltd, 1961) 17-19.
[23] Raymond E. Brown, *The Gospel According to John (Volume 1)* (London: Geoffrey Chapman, 1966) 439.

Christians within the framework of conscious creation of a Christian socio-theological environment formed the essential foundation of the Gospel of John.

This is nowhere more clear than in John 11:45-54. Bultmann, Dodd, and Brown all agree on the idea of this pasaage faulting the Jews in the context of the early Christian conflict with non-Christian Jews. Bultmann portrays Jews as blind, but Dodd notes that this text meant to condemn Jews for more deliberate plotting. Brown takes a more positivistic view in emphasizing the Christian affirmation of Jesus' redemptive work and legitimization of the new faith community. All agree, however, that this pericope in John meant to emphasize the separation between Judaism and Christianity. I would affirm that this pericope indicates the Christian milieu of the Johannine text and that the Christian milieu was central and causative in nature in text creation. This is evident when we examine the content and literary structure of the pericope. The Gospel writer exhibits his personal apologetic concerns. We can detect 3 layers: (1) oracle, (2) narrative, (3) redaction. There is a prophetic oracle supposedly preserved; namely, the idea that Jesus was to die and that his death would bring ingathering. On the one hand, it is irrelevant whether this oracle goes back to the earliest strata of event-transmission. The most important element is that the idea of ingathering is clear. It is the most clear form of ingathering idea found in the Gospel of John. Most probably, this oracle goes back to the earliest times because in light of the whole of the Gospel of John, this oracle seems a bit out of place. Although there are indirect references to ingathering, there are not many direct references to ingathering as we find here. But perhaps more relevant and certainly most poignant is the idea that Jesus' death is central to ingathering. This is certainly opposed to the traditional notion of ingathering. Further digression exhibits itself in the oracle. It seems to indicate that Gentiles are included in the ingathering. The inclusive language stands opposed to the rather exclusive ingathering found in the traditional formula. The emphasis on including Gentiles for redemptive ingathering is consistent with the teaching in the Gospel of John, redefining "the children of God" as those who believe, regardless of ethnicity.

  Within the pericope found in John, this positive association of the inclusiveness of the people of God is coupled with negative attack on the traditional formula. The attack takes the form of portraying Jews as guilty in murdering the divine ingatherer. By the virtue of the fact that Jews kill Jesus, the text implies that they have no right to be ingathered; they have forfeited their right.

One sees here that the Christian apologetic concern rising out of a distinctively (and self-consciously) defining Christian milieu played the crucial role in the final literary product of this pericope. One can see how assuming a Jewish or Hellenistic milieu would be misleading. If, in fact, a Jewish milieu was the socio-theological milieu out of which this text arose, it would be difficult to understand (1) the lack of more integrated use of the ingathering formula, (2) extreme polemic against Jews, (3) not a more explicit push for inclusion of Gentiles. In other words, there was no need to develop the ingathering formula further, because the community to which this Gospel was being addressed was not familiar with the traditional ingathering formula. Secondly, extreme polemic against Jews was possible because this text was being composed primarily for the in-group. The apologetic concern was not for engageing the Jews in intellectual battle per se but rather for strengthening the Christian community. The Christian milieu, and not a Jewish milieu, would allow such activity. Third, the author did not need to push for inclusion of Gentiles because the Christian milieu out of which this composition arose already was composed of Jews and Gentiles who converted to Christianity. Any teaching of the children of God being members of the faith community was for didactic and apologetic concerns. Given the reality of the Christian milieu, a specific, isolated push for Gentile inclusion was unnecessary.

One can see that this pericope did not rise out of a distinctively Hellenistic milieu because (1) Jewish history in the pericope is recounted in language that is not Hellenistic (although not distinctively Jewish), (2) Prophecy seems to deny the necessity of the piety of the speaker, which is a concept foreign to a Hellenistic milieu, (3) ingathering concept presupposed in John is dependent on ingathering in the Old Testament. In other words, certain familiarity with Biblical history and character of the Jewish council is assumed. The most likely reason for this is that those in the community understood the Jewish council as the political body that condemned Jesus to death. This memory-preservation served an apologetic purpose in the Christian community. Secondly, the concept of prophecy embodied in the pericope militates against a non-Christian Hellenistic milieu. Christian tradition had a traitor among the inner circle of the apostles of Christ. There was an implicit understanding that humans are fallible and God works through even the condemned (like Judas Ischariot). This would not have worked in Hellenistic culture. The bearer of the oracle had to be worthy of the oracle. This illustrates that the writer operated from a distinctively

Christian milieu. Thirdly, there is a lack of Old Testament-type ingathering concept in Hellenistic tradition. The ingathering concept as reformulated in John is presupposing and reshaping Old Testament's traditional formula of ingathering. Even if the writer understood the concept, a non-Christian audience would have been lost. This all indicates that the Gospel writer wrote in a distinctively Christian milieu with presumptions innate to such a milieu.

## Syntactical and Semantic Consideration of בעוד[1]

In the Hebrew Bible בעוד functions as a guiding factor in a temporal clause, and thus it is translated as such: "while" or "when." Surprisingly, however, this form has not received much attention.[2] Perhaps, this is due to the fact that the temporal force of בעוד is understood analogously to the temporal force of עוד in its usage with a participle, as is by Eduard König.[3] Yet,

---

[1] This paper was delivered at the 1997 Central States SBL/ASOR Meeting in Kansas City, Missouri, while I was a Lady Davis Fellow at the Hebrew University of Jerusalem. I would like to thank the Lady Davis Trust for funding me for the costs of travel and attendance of the academic conference. Also, I would like to thank Professor Avi Hurvitz of the Hebrew University of Jerusalem for providing helpful comments on this paper.

[2] Most books on Biblical Hebrew grammar ignore this form. Even some books on Hebrew syntax fail to mention this form even in passing. For a worthy treatment of the form, see Eduard König, <u>Historisch-kritisches lehrgebäude der hebräischen Sprache: Syntax</u> (Leipzig: J. C. Hinrichs'sche Buchhandlung, 1897) §§ 401m, q, x; 409f.

[3] König writes concerning בעוד הילד חי in 2 Sam 12:22: "Nach der Analogie des עוד ist בעוד construirt..." (§ 409f). On the temporal force of עוד with participle, see also <u>Gesenius' Hebrew Grammar as Edited and</u>

there is a significant syntactical difference between the עוד + participle constructions and constructions guided by בעוד.

In the first construction, עוד is secondary or even peripheral; the participle alone is capable of the temporal force.[4] It can even be argued that עוד is an enclitic particle used for emphasis on the force of the participle in the עוד + participle constructions.[5] An example of this particular use of עוד in a temporal clause motivated by a participle is found in Isa 65:24. One finds, עוד הם מדברים ואני אשמע, and this is translated, "While they are yet speaking, I will hear." One sees that the

---

Enlarged by the Late E. Kautzsch, second English edition revised by A., E. Cowley (Oxford: Clarendon Press, 1910) § 164; S. R. Driver, A Treatise on the Use of the Tenses in Hebrew and Some Other Syntactical Questions (Oxford: Clarendon Press, 1892) § 169; H. Bauer and P. Leander, Historische Grammatik der hebräischen Sprache des alten Testaments (Halle: Verlag von Max Niemeyer, 1922) § 80w; and Abba Bendavid, Biblical Hebrew and Mishnaic Hebrew [in Hebrew] (Tel Aviv: Dvir Co. Ltd. 1971) § 346.

[4]This force of the participle is also extant in other languages, such as the genitive absolute in Greek and the ablative absolute in Latin.

[5]Thus, Bruce K. Waltke and M. O'Connor write in An Introduction to Biblical Hebrew Syntax (Winona Lake: Eisenbrauns, 1990): "Sometimes, the adverb עוד is used with the participle to emphasize the simultaneity. More often, the participle describes an ongoing state of affairs, involving repeated or continuous action" (§ 37:6d).

participle is the primary factor in the temporal clause.

On the other hand, בעוד is a primary, even essential, element in the construction guided by it. It is the my argument that בעוד functions as a status constructus, and the following elements function in the absolute state. And the syntactically construct edifice guided by בעוד functions semantically as a temporal clause.

Carl Brockelmann perceives the genitival force of בעוד in 2 Sam 12:22 (בעוד הילד חי) and points to this as an example of Genetivsatz. Brockelmann's translation, "solange das Kind lebendig war,"[6] is helpful in that it takes into account the predicate adjectival force of חי and the temporal semantic force of בעוד. It is unfortunate, however, that his exposition on the subject of its genitival character is limited to his translation, and one is left to infer from his translation. Constructions guided by בעוד, in fact, provide a consistent picture of the syntactically construct usage of the form and its semantic acceptance of the force of subordinating conjunction with the denotation of "when" or "while."

In fact, בעוד has almost a prepositional force analogous to לפני (particle ל joined to the noun פנים in construct, which as

---

[6]Carl Brockelmann, Hebräische Syntax (Neukirchen Kreis Moers: Berlag der Buchhandlung des Erziehungsvereins, 1956) 141 (§ 144).

a prepositional unit is followed by a noun or unit in the absolute state). These בעוד constructions, therefore, may be translated literally as "in the continuance of..."[7] and the context will then provide the precise translation of the phrase. There are twenty constructions guided by בעוד in the Bible, and they can be divided into three groups. First group consists of בעוד followed by a noun and its attributive adjectives. Second group is more complex than the first one in that בעוד is not only followed by a unit consisting of noun and its attributes, but also by a third unit beginning with a prepositional particle and descriptive of the second unit. Third group of constructions guided by בעוד consists of בעוד followed by a noun, or pronominal suffix, and a participle, either explicit or implied,

---

[7]See the entry עוד (especially, the subheading of בעוד) in F. Brown, S. R. Driver, and Ch. A. Briggs, <u>A Hebrew and English Lexicon of the Old Testament</u> (Oxford: Clarendon Press, 1907) 728-729. Here, עוד is defined as a substantive with the meaning, "a going around, continuance," but it is shown often to be used adverbially as "still, yet, again, besides." The original substantival use of עוד is often assumed. In Paul Joüon's <u>A Grammar of Biblical Hebrew</u>, translated and revised by T. Muraoka (Rome: Editrice Pontificio Istituto Biblico, 1993), the substantival character of עוד is considered in its treatment as an adverb: "One may note that עוֹד, which is probably in origin a substantive (<u>repetition, continuation</u>)..." (§ 102k).

functioning with the force of a predicative adjective.

There are ten occurrences in the Bible that belong to the first group: Gen 40:13; Gen 40:19; Josh 1:11; 2 Sam 3:35; Isa 7:8; Isa 21:16; Jer 15:9; Jer 28:3; Jer 28:11; and Prov 31:15. The first group, being composed of two units, is the most simple of the three groups. בעוד, or the first unit, is composed of the particle ב plus the substantive עוד in the construct, and the second unit that follows is an absolute noun or an absolute noun with its attributive adjectives composing an absolute substantival unit. This syntactically construct unit finds semantic reality of a temporal clause. For example, בעוד היום in 2 Sam 3:35, which is translated literally as "in the continuance of that day," realizes the semantic force of the temporal clause in the freer rendition, "while it was yet day" (cf. Jer 15:9).

Not all of the ten attestations in the first group indicate concurrent temporal state, however. In fact, some בעוד constructions in this category indicate a future conditional temporal state. Thus, more difficult to translate is בעוד שלשת ימים in Gen 40:13 and Gen 40:9. Literally, it is translated, "in the continuance of three days." In light of contextual and semantic considerations, however, it is more freely rendered, "when it will be three days" or "when three days have passed." The freer translation guided by the temporal semantic force of בעוד takes the verb יצא into consideration. The future force of the verb dominates the denotative content of the simple בעוד construction.

But syntactically, both בעוד constructions that find contemporaneous semantic reality or future conditional temporal semantic content are the same. They are composed of two units: the first unit with the particle ב is joined to the substantive עוד in the construct, followed by the second substantive unit in the absolute state. It is important to note that to the users of the language, the distinction in translation that we require in light of the context might not have been necessary.

There are four attestations in the Bible of the second group, which, as an extension of the first group, has a third element in addition to the בעוד + noun (and its attributive adjective) component. These four attestations are found in Gen 48:7; Amos 4:7; Ps 39:2; and Job 29:5. The third unit, which qualifies the second unit, starts with a prepositional word or particle followed by an infinitive as in Gen 48:7 (לבא), by a noun as in Amos 4:7 (לקציר), or by a pronominal suffix as in Ps 39:2 (לנגדי).

One may render the constructions in this group as extended status constructus. Thus, one translates literally the phrase in

Gen 48:7 (בעוד כברת־ארץ לבא אפרתא) as "in the continuance of little way to come to Efrat." One sees that the third unit, לבא אפרתא, qualifies the second unit, כברת־ארץ. The third unit, therefore, answers the question, "a little way to what?" Since בעוד constructions have the semantic force of a temporal clause, this phrase would be more freely translated as "while there was yet a little way to come to Efrat."

In group three, one finds six attestations in the Hebrew Bible: Gen 25:6; Deut 31:27; 2 Sam 12:22; Isa 28:4; Ps 104:33; and Ps 146:2. In fact, there is only one example from the Bible of this construction without the affixed pronominal suffix; namely, 2 Sam 12:22 (בעוד הילד חי). This is translated literally as "in the continuance of the child living." This syntactically faithful rendering finds semantic reality as a temporal clause, and, therefore, it is more freely translated as "while the child was yet alive."

One notices that בעוד...חי is formulaic in this group; excepting Isa 28:4, all the examples in this group have this denotation. Gen 25:6 has בעודנו חי, which is literally translated, "in the continuance of him living," and more freely rendered, "while he was yet living." Deut 31:27 has בעודני חי עמכם היום, which is literally translated, "in the continuance of me living with you this day," and more freely rendered, "while I am yet living with you this day."

Although Ps 104:33 and Ps 146:2 have בעודי without חי, this has the same denotative force as other examples. Thus, בעודי is rendered "in the continuance of me (living)," or more freely, "while I am yet living." One possible explanation for the absence of חי is that it became superfluous by the stage of Biblical Hebrew in which the passages in the Psalms are found. Thus, בעוד + suffix is an idiomatic way of expressing concurrent existence of the person or object that the suffix modifies with or without the adjectival factor denoting that reality.

There is only one attestation in this third category that does not refer to human life. Yet, it is worthy to note that even this reference describes a concurrent existence, albeit of an object rather than a person. בעודה בכפו is found in Isa 28:4 and is a בעוד + suffix construction. This is literally translated as "in the continuance of it (existing) in his hand" and is more freely translated as "while it is yet in his hand."

Looking at the three groups of בעוד constructions above, one sees that they function as <u>status constructus</u> syntactically with the semantic force of a temporal clause. The construction existed in the earliest stages of the Hebrew language and continued, even developing an idiomatic expression based on it. Yet, in the later stages of

Biblical Hebrew, this construction fades as a key player in the semantically temporal clause.

This phenomena is paralleled in the extra-biblical sources. One sees among the extant sources that the בעוד construction is found in the pre-exilic period, but not in non-biblical sources belonging to the Late Biblical Hebrew stage of the Hebrew language.

Among the pre-exilic Hebrew sources, one finds in the Siloam tunnel inscription an attestation of a בעוד construction[8] belonging to the second of the three groups that were presented earlier in this paper. The construction, found in line two, reads [ובעוד שלש אמת להנ[קב.[9] As in attestations in the Hebrew Bible belonging to the second group, one finds here the first unit בעוד followed by a nominative unit

---

[8]There is another attestation of the word בעוד in line one, but parts needed to complete the בעוד construction is missing from the inscription.

[9]The reconstruction of להנקב finds agreement in G. A. Cooke, A Text-Book of North-Semitic Inscriptions (Oxford: Clarendon Press, 1903) 15; S. R. Driver, Notes on the Hebrew Text and the Topography of the Book of Samuel (Oxford: Clarendon Press, 1913) ix; H. Donner and W. Röllig, Kanaanäische und aramäische Inschriften, Band 1: Texte (Wiesbaden: Otto Harrassowitz, 1966) 189; E. Peuch, "L'inscription du Tunnel de Siloé," RB 81 (1974) 197; John C. L. Gibson, Textbook of Syrian Semitic Inscriptions, Volume 1: Hebrew and Moabite Inscriptions (Oxford: Clarendon Press, 1971) 22.

(namely, שלש אמת), which in turn is followed by a third unit (להנ[קב]) which is qualitative of the second unit. This בעוד construction is literally translated as "in the continuance of three cubits to be bored through." In light of the semantic force of בעוד to characterize its construction as a temporal clause, it is more freely rendered as "while there was yet three cubits to be bored through." This occurrence in the Siloam tunnel inscription provides multiple attestation of the בעוד construction in the pre-exilic period in an extra-biblical source.

Yet, the claim to multiple attestation of בעוד construction cannot be made to extra-biblical Hebrew corpus belonging to the post-exilic period. When one looks at Qumran documents, one notices the conspicuous absence of the בעוד constructions. In his concordance, Charlesworth lists forty-eight occurrences of עוד and two occurrences of עוד + pronominal suffix,[10] but none of בעוד. More enlightening is the fact that many collections of Dead Sea Scrolls are also simply missing עוד. A case in point is volume ten in the Discoveries in the Judaean Desert series. In <u>Qumran 4: Miqsat</u>

---

[10] James H. Charlesworth (with R. E. Whitaker, L. G. Hickerson, S. R. A. Starbuck, L. T. Struckenbruck), <u>Graphic Concordance to the Dead Sea Scrolls</u> (Tübingen: J. C. B. Mohr; Louisville: Westminster/ John Knox Press, 1991)

Ma'a'se Ha-Torah.[11] neither בעוד nor עוד exists in the whole corpus contained therein.

Even those occurrences of עוד in the Dead Sea Scroll corpus show that their function in the semantic context of a temporal clause is basically obsolete. For instance, one finds seven attestations of עוד in The Temple Scroll.[12] Yigael Yadin translates all of them as particles with denotation of "again, still, yet" and takes none of them as functioning in the context of a temporal clause.

The Book of Ben Sira is likewise conspicuous in its absence of בעוד and בעוד constructions. As in the case of the Dead Sea Scrolls, the Book of Ben Sira does, however, have attestations of עוד. There are nine attestations of it without the pronominal suffix and three attestations with affixed pronominal suffix.[13] All these function as particles.

Thus, Abba Bendavid notes that the Biblical Hebrew (בעוד(הילד חי construction is parallel to Mishnaic Hebrew constructions

---

[11] Elisha Qimron and John Strugnell, Qumran 4: Miqsat Ma'a'se Ha-Torah (Oxford: Clarendon Press, 1994).

[12] Yigael Yadin (ed.), The Temple Scroll (Volume 2: Text and Commentary) (Jerusalem: The Israel Exploration Society, 1983).

[13] The Book of Ben Sira: Text, Concordance and an Analysis of the Vocabulary (Jerusalem: The Academy of the Hebrew Language and the Shrine of the Book, 1973) 234.

guided by בזמן ש and עד ש.[14] M. H. Segal in Grammar of Mishnaic Hebrew also agrees that these are the primary guiders of temporal clauses. In light of this, it is no surprise that one does not find בעוד constructions in the extra-biblical sources in the period of Late Biblical Hebrew; בעוד has been replaced by another temporal clause marker.

In conclusion, בעוד constructions, although previously not given proper treatment, show themselves to be significant in the study of the Hebrew language. To identify בעוד constructions as merely analogous to עוד + participle constructions would not only be limiting for understanding temporal clauses in the Hebrew language, but, more importantly, it would simply be inaccurate.

In the context of the history of the Hebrew language, בעוד constructions emerge as early grammatical constructs, finding multiple attestation in Classical Biblical Hebrew texts as well as a pre-exilic Hebrew inscription, namely the Siloam tunnel inscription. This semantic function of בעוד constructions as temporal clauses continued into Late Biblical Hebrew as is seen in the attestations, such as that of Prov 31:15. Its evolutionary (and diminishing) nature can

---

[14]Bendavid 265. Also, see M. H. Segal, Grammar of Mishnaic Hebrew (Oxford: Clarendon Press, 1927) § 513.

be seen in the formulization of בעוד...חי, which comes to drop the חי in the book of Psalms, where בעוד + pronominal suffix, such as בעודי, translates into "while I am yet alive." The diminishing nature of בעוד in Late Biblical Hebrew is further affirmed by its absence in the representative biblical books of Chronicles, Ezra, and Nehemiah.

The cessation of בעוד constructions is confirmed by its absence in the whole of extant Dead Sea Scrolls and the book of Ben Sira. Furthermore, its absence and linguistic replacement by such temporal clauses guided by בזמן ש in Mishnaic Hebrew literature further affirm the discontinued usage of בעוד constructions.

One possible and constructive way of looking at the development of בעוד constructions is to view בעוד as a linear development from the earlier substantive עוד and to see this development as paralleling the development of עוד as a particle within various grammatical situations, including עוד + participle constructions with similar temporal clause semantic force. This approach is helpful for understanding the anatomy of the syntax of בעוד constructions, which belong to status constructus, and is also useful for studying the syntactical nature and semantic function of temporal clauses in general.

## Ancient Inscriptions and the Study of Biblical Hebrew[*]

The inscriptions in the pre-exilic period play a significant role in affirming the existence of Hebrew at least as a literary language in that period. Inscriptions display parallel existence to Biblical Hebrew. Although questions regarding canonization and transmission (along with issues of redaction and editing) surround the questions regarding the history of Biblical Hebrew, inscriptions provide a solid evidence for the diachronic development of Biblical Hebrew before the exile.

The inscriptions relevant to this study can be divided into northern Hebrew inscriptions and southern Hebrew inscriptions. Among the northern Hebrew[1] inscrip-

---

[*] This paper represents intensive research conducted on the history of the Hebrew language under the guidance of Israel's leading Hebrew linguist, Professor Avi Hurvitz of the Hebrew University of Jerusalem from 1995 to 1997.

[1] Rendsburg prefers the term "Israelian" over the term "Northern Hebrew," because he believes that the latter term seems to point to those regions in the far north, such as the tribal territories of Dan, Asher, Naphtali. Rendsburg, therefore, believes that the term "Israelian," first introduced by H. L. Ginsberg to

tions can be included the Gezer Calendar, the Samaria ostraca, a stele fragment from Samaria, and ostraca from Tell Qasile and Beth Shean. And among the southern inscriptions can be included Siloam inscriptions, the Arad ostraca and Lachish letters, a letter from Mesad Hasharyahu (or Yavneh Yam), Khirbet El-Qom inscriptions, papyrus from Wadi Murabbaat, Kuntillet Ajrud inscriptions, and Khirbet Beit Lei inscriptions.

The Gezer Calendar is dated to the tenth century BC. It contains dialectal and archaic features and is the only inscription from this early period.[2] This leads Ian Young to speculate about the inscription's existence before the standardization of Biblical Hebrew. Young states: "The Gezer Calendar is the only inscription from this early period, perhaps thus dating from before the royal standard language (Standard Biblical Hebrew) fully established itself as

---

refer to the Northern Kingdom, better describes the "non-Judahite variety of Hebrew," which finds grammatical attestation in stories from central regions, such as territories of Ephraim and of Reuben, which are essentially on the same latitude as Judah (Gary A. Rendsburg, "Morphological Evidence for Regional Dialects in Ancient Hebrew," *Linguistics and Biblical Hebrew*, ed. Walter R. Bodine (Winona Lake: Eisenbrauns, 1992, pp. 65-88) 69-70).

[2] Ian Young, *Diversity in Pre-Exilic Hebrew* (Tübingen: J. C. B. Mohr (Paul Siebeck), 1993) 118-119.

the normative type of the High form of the Hebrew language."[3] Eduard Kutscher, while affirming the inscription's tenth century date, takes the speculation further than Young's perception of the inscription's place in the early stages of the standardization of Biblical Hebrew. Kutscher, in fact, questions whether it would be appropriate to classify the Gezer Calendar as belonging to Hebrew. Kutscher states: "the Gezer calendar ... has grammatical peculiarities not found in BH. It is questionable whether it should even be considered as belonging to Hebrew. (Gezer, situated in the Philistine plain, did not always belong to the Judean kingdom)."[4] Yet, Kutscher goes onto state: "The vocabulary of the inscriptions is practically identical with that of BH and only a few new roots turn up."[5] This shows that Kutscher essentially recognizes the Gezer calendar as Hebrew. In fact, Kutscher concludes: "It is mainly the possibility of the existence of an Israelite (northern) dialect, as distinct from the Judean (southern) dialect which intrigues scholars."[6] The existence of divergence is not too surprising in light of the historical event in which

---

[3] Young 119.
[4] Eduard Yechezkel Kutscher, *A History of the Hebrew Language*, ed. Raphael Kutscher (Jerusalem: The Magnes Press (The Hebrew University), 1982) 67.
[5] Kutscher 67.
[6] Kutscher 70.

Gezer was given to Solomon only in the mid-tenth century BC.[7] Yet, the inclusion of the Gezer inscription in the corpus of Hebrew literature cannot be denied. Angel Sáenz-Badillos affirms: "The Gezer tablet ... employs forms and characteristics of northern Hebrew."[8]

One notable feature in the Gezer Calendar that has raised much debate is the word *yrhw*. Cross and Freedman in *Early Hebrew Orthography* argue that the *waw* is consonantal and represents the third masculine singular pronominal suffix attached to a dual noun and should be pronounced *ew*. Two other possible explanations are that the *waw* represents an archaic nominative dual construct *o*, or *aw*, or that the *waw* is an archaic nominative plural construct *u*. Ziony Zevit finds all these explanations problematic and speculates the possibility that it might be a *matres lectionis*.[9] The word *yrhw* continues to raise academic debate as does the Gezer Calender itself.

The Samaria ostraca is dated to the eighth century BC, although precise dating is in dispute. Kutscher,[10] Tigay,[11] and

---

[7] Young 117.
[8] Angel Sáenz-Badillos, *A History of the Hebrew Language*, tr. John Elwolde (Cambridge: Cambridge University Press, 1993) 64.
[9] Ziony Zevit, <u>Matres Lectionis</u> in Ancient Hebrew Epigraphs (Cambridge: American Schools of Oriental Research, 1980) 6.
[10] Kutscher 64.

Aharoni date it in the early eighth century BC, while Cross dates it in late eighth century BC.[12] The purpose of the ostraca is under dispute, although its discovery in the royal palace in Samaria leads some scholars to assume it as the work of a menial scribe using the Hebrew language in the most basic administrative form. Young asserts: "By definition we are dealing with eighth century official Samaria Hebrew."[13]

Some have remarked that the Official Northern Hebrew of the Samaria Ostraca shows a few isoglosses with Phoenician as against Biblical Hebrew. For example, *satt*[14] for 'year' is used instead of the Biblical *sanah*. Young believes that this is an example of a relic of the Phoenician dominance of the North during the Omride dynasty in the ninth century Israel, in which King Ahab's wife Jezebel, a Tyrian princess, brought with her the prestige of Phoenician culture, as evidenced in the large scale devotion, at least among the upper classes, to the Tyrian Baal (1 Kings 16:23ff. and the Elijah Stories). The Samaria Ostraca, as Young dates, comes from about fifty years after the end of the Omride dynasty. Young

---

[11] Jeffrey H. Tigay, *You Shall Have No Other Gods: Israelite Religion in the Light of Hebrew Inscriptions* (Atlanta: Scholars Press, 1986) 9.
[12] Young 114.
[13] Young 114.
[14] Kutscher remarks that this form looks "suspiciously Aramaic" (66).

believes that during the time of Jezebel, Phoenicianisms in official circles might have been considered a good form.[15]

A stele fragment from Samaria containing three letters [*'sr*], has been dated to the mid-eighth century. There is a clear divider after the *resh*, which led Sukenik to claim that the word is *'aser* ("who, which"). The word belonged to the first line of the stele, which would fit into a phrase such as "the stele *which* X king of Israel erected." This inscription, as a part of official or monumental inscription, is significant in that it uses *'aser*, which was the High literary form, paralleled in the form *se-* among some biblical works with Northern dialectal flavor.[16]

Two ostraca from Tell Qasile, dated to the eighth century, and a fragmentary ostracon from Beth Shean, dated to the ninth-eighth centuries are significant in that they provide a *plene* spelling of *byt*, in distinction to the Samaria Ostraca. Distant location of the two sites -- Tell Qasile being an Israelite port in the Mediterranean coast and Beth Shean being far inland -- raises in Young's mind doubts regarding the general tendency in the North to diphthong contraction, especially as it pertains to the *ay*-diphthong. Young considers two possibilities. First, the reduced diphthong was writ-

---

[15] Young 29.
[16] Young 115-116.

ten *plene* with historical spelling. Second, the diphthong was not contracted.[17] The writer prefers the first explanation with some modification. Not only is there *ay*-diphthong reduction, the medial *yod* is a *mater lectionis* of that reduction, and not merely a historical spelling.

Northern Hebrew inscriptions having been considered, southern Hebrew inscriptions will now find their attention. The Siloam inscriptions are dated to the end of the eighth century.[18] The inscriptions were found on the wall of the tunnel connecting the Virgin's Spring to the Pool of Siloam in Jerusalem. Scholars identify this tunnel as the tunnel that Hezekiah built for the sake of water supply of Jerusalem in the wake of an imminent attack from the Assyrian king Sennacherib in 701 BC (2 Kings 20:20; 2 Chronicles 32:2-4, 30).[19]

The similarity of the inscriptions with Biblical Hebrew does raise some speculation that Biblical Hebrew was spoken in the period of the Siloam inscriptions. Young, however, prefers the idea that the similarity is due to commonality of tradition; Standard Biblical Hebrew prose is a national literary language and the inscriptions represent a less literary national standard. In arguing thus, Young dismisses the

---

[17] Young 116.
[18] Kutscher 64.
[19] Young 103.

theory that Biblical Hebrew was spoken at the time and asserts that this dismissal is "well recognized" now.[20]

There are two inscriptions -- namely, "Siloam Tomb" inscriptions -- from a tomb near Jerusalem, which are dated paleographically to roughly the same period as the Siloam Tunnel inscriptions. Since the second inscription is extremely fragmentary, the first funerary inscription is the more significant one. Because the owner of the inscription is identified as a high royal officer, the expectation is for Jerusalem Official Hebrew of the highest order. Indeed, there are no *waw*-consecutive forms. *byt* and *'yn* are written with the medial *yod*. Also, the inscription uniformly uses *-h* as the third person masculine singular suffix. However, the third sentence of the inscription starts with the word *'rwr* ("accursed").[21] Although this is a standard curse formula, the *waw* is a *plene* spelling.

The Arad ostraca is dated to the beginning of the sixth century, before the end of the kingdom of Judah.[22] The Arad ostraca comes from the Eastern Negev, some twenty-six kilometers east of Beersheba. Arad, at that time, was a Judean mili-

---

[20] Young 104. Dismissing the possibility that Biblical Hebrew was spoken is premature and lacks preponderance of evidence.
[21] Young 107-108.
[22] Kutscher 64.

tary fortress protecting the area against the Edomites. Although contemporaneous with Lachish letters, the Arad ostraca exhibits a greater diversity of style.[23]

Two notable "aberrant" characteristics of the Arad ostraca are the intrusion of the *waw* consecutive, which can be seen as the personal style of the writer, and the phonetic change of *p* to *b* in text twenty-four, which can be seen as a dialectal variation.[24]

Lachish letters are dated approximately to the same period as the Arad ostraca in the beginning of the sixth century.[25] The twenty-one ostraca were discovered in a small room under the gate tower of the site of Tell ed-Duweir, thought to be the site of ancient Lachish.[26] Young notes that the ostraca from Lachish, like those from Samaria, were the script of professional second grade scribes, since the job of noting delivery of produce or of writing the correspondence of a garrison commander in the Judean army would be the job of junior scribes rather than the senior scribes employed in the service of the King, Temple, or courts of law.[27] Young states:

---

[23] Young 111.
[24] Young 112-113.
[25] Kutscher 64.
[26] Young 110.
[27] Young 99.

"These letters must represent true 'Official Hebrew.'"[28]

The letter from Mesad Hasharyahu, or Yavneh Yam, is dated to the end of the seventh century during the days of Josiah.[29] Young fixes a date around 630 BC for the ostracon, which was found in the remains of an ancient fortress situated on the coast, west of Gezer. Judean law is the background to the legal dispute, and the letters show that they were written by a practical hand. The lack of linguistic skill exhibited by the author, especially repetitions and badly formed sentences, has surprised the commentators.[30]

One noticeable feature of the Yavneh Yam inscription is the existence of the *waw* consecutive construction in at least four places. This stands in contrast to the characteristics of Official Hebrew, as is found in the likes of the Siloam Tunnel inscription.[31]

Inscriptions from Khirbet El-Qom, which is located near Lachish and Khirbet Beit Lei, were found in burial caves dating from ninth to sixth centuries BC. First two inscriptions, dated to the seventh century BC, are short funerary inscriptions containing basically the name of the occupants

---

[28] Young 110.
[29] Kutscher 64.
[30] Young 120.
[31] Young 120-121.

of the tomb. The third inscription, dated between 750 to 700 BC, is from the pillar of a burial cave and is more significant. There is a wide reading of this inscription. Some, like Dever, describe it as a graffito, not carefully nor deeply incised. Others, like Young, point out that its being written in a burial cave points to a wealthier, more educated element of society. In regards to style, the inscription has straightforward style and syntax, which, Young believes, is indicative of Official Hebrew in contrast to the Literary Hebrew of the Bible. In this inscription, the third person masculine singular suffix is uniformly -$h$.[32]

The papyrus palimpsest from Wadi Murabbaat is dated to the first half of the seventh century BC. Here contains a crudely penned list of names over an elegantly written letter. Unfortunately, there are only two incompletely preserved lines. There are no specifically literary features. Worthy of mention is the familiar "and now" ($w$ '$t$), which can be found in Official letters.[33]

The Kuntillet Ajrud inscriptions are dated between the ninth and eighth centuries. Kuntillet Ajrud was a religious site in eastern Sinai, inhabited solely by priests giving blessing to travelers journeying to the South. The main deity involved is YHWH of Teman or YHWH of Samaria.

---

[32] Young 108-109.
[33] Young 113.

The full corpus of texts from Kuntillet Ajrud still requires careful sifting once it becomes available, and individual authors have to be examined extensively. Yet, the fact that the inscriptions came from a cross-section of the divided kingdom but display only little divergence from Standard Hebrew shows that a century after the Gezer calendar, Standard Hebrew has gained wide acceptance and usage throughout the former empire of Solomon.[34]

The graffiti of Khirbet Beit Lei were found in an ancient burial cave near Lachish and are dated to the sixth century. There is disagreement as to their actual reading. Neveh see them as similar to Psalms, while Cross hold them to be prophecy in a classical poetic form. Yet, significant is the fact that the inscriptions are a classical literary Hebrew poetry of some sort.[35]

Although there are dialectal differences among Hebrew inscriptions, the inscriptions as a whole exhibit general characteristics. One notable characteristic is the tendency toward defective spelling, especially in medial positions. But there are several words which are spelled *plene*, such as *ywtr* ("more") and *mws'* ("source").[36] These examples not only show *plene* spelling but also provide a picture into the

---

[34] Young 119.
[35] Young 121.
[36] Kutscher 65.

general tendency of the Hebrew inscriptions toward diphthong reduction.

Some scholars, such as Sáenz-Badillos,[37] believe that the *waw* on these words were still pronounced as consonants and argued that the original diphthongs to which the Hebrew /o:/ went back had not contracted in this period in Judea in contradistinction to the diphthong contraction in Northern Hebrew. Garr agrees with Sáenz-Badillos' position that the diphthongs were contracted in Northern Hebrew but not in Southern Hebrew. Garr states: "Northern Hebrew thus followed the pattern of diphthong contraction already evident in Ugaritic and in the Amarna letters from north Palestine."[38] Garr continues and comments on the situation of diphthong reduction in Southern Hebrew: "These diphthongs were uncontracted in both medial, and presumably final, positions."[39]

Kutscher believes that this assumption was faulty, because in the Siloam inscription, one finds the word *ywm* ("day") spelled defectively without the *waw*. Since the /o:/ in the word goes back to an original diphthong, this case indicates that the diphthong had already contracted. Young agrees

---

[37] Sáenz-Badillos 66.
[38] W. Randall Garr, *Dialect Geography of Syria-Palestine, 1000 - 586 B.C.E.* (Philadelphia: University of Pennsylvania Press, 1985) 38.
[39] Garr 39.

with Kutscher: "On the basis of *ym* and *ql* the diphthong *aw* had undergone a general reduction."[40] This contraction points to the contraction of diphthong also in *ywtr* ("more") and *mws'* ("source"). Thus, the *waw* should be considered a plene spelling of /o:/.[41] *Plene* spelling, in general, is characteristic of the Hebrew of the period. Young notes: "The historical tendency in the Hebrew tradition is toward *plene* spelling."[42]

Garr does recognize that *ywm* ("day") was possibly contracted in Southern Hebrew and sees it as one of the two exceptions in Southern Hebrew, whose diphthong Garr characterized as non-contracting. The form *ym* (for "day") appears throughout the Southern Hebrew texts from the late eighth century BC (Siloam Tunnel) to the early sixth century BCE (Lachish, Arad)[43] and the form comparative to *yawm* in Old Aramaic and Ammonite, never appears. Garr provides two possibilities. The first

---

[40] Young 107. But it must be noted that Young questions whether the *aw*-diphthong reduction was characteristic of Official Hebrew. Young prefers to see the two forms as dialectal forms which have gained acceptance in Official Hebrew. Young believes that the *aw*-diphthong is, otherwise, "generally retained" and the *ay*-diphthong is "retained in all positions" (199).
[41] Kutscher 65.
[42] Young 24.
[43] Young 106.

explanation is that the "defective" form *ym*, at one time, found parallel existence as a singular to the Biblical Hebrew singular for "day," namely *ywm*. Garr bases his argument on the premise that there were two Biblical Hebrew form for "day"; namely, *\*yawm > ywm* (*yôm*) and *\*yam > ymym* (*yamim*) / *ymy* (*yamê*).[44] Garr's explanation is significantly weakened, if not refuted, in light of the reality that the plural forms for "day" are used by analogy to the plural forms for "year," whose absolute form is *snym* and construct form is *sny*. This is evident in the two examples found in Deuteronomy 32:7 and Psalms 90:15, in which the poetic plural construct forms of *ymy* for "days" and *sny* for "years" find parallel attestation.[45]

Joüon-Muraoka does mention in the notes that it may be possible that the form and *ym* could have existed side by side for "day," as Garr explained. Joüon-Muraoka bases the argument in light of the attestation of *ym* in the Siloam inscriptions and other early Hebrew epigraphic materials, and in Phoenician and Ugaritic. Joüon-Muraoka further mention that Epigraphic South Arabian attests to *ym* and *ywm*.[46] Yet, the

---

[44] Garr 39.
[45] Paul Joüon-T. Muraoka, *A Grammar of Biblical Hebrew* (Rome: Editrice Pontificio Istituto Biblico, 1993) 320.
[46] Joüon-Muraoka 320.

examples that Joüon-Muraoka provide are not very strong, since they support examples of contraction. The writer will now leave the Hebrew inscriptions aside in this case since they are argued and shown in this paper as examples of contraction, the possibility of which is not clearly refuted, even by Garr. Actually, as is seen in Garr's second explanation for the attestation of *ym* in Southern Hebrew, Garr actually considers it as indicative of diphthong contraction, albeit imported into Southern Hebrew.[47]

As regards to Phoenician, it exhibits the reduction of the diphthong *aw* > *o* and *ay* > *e*.[48] Garr, also, agrees and states that the first millennium Phoenician dialects contracted diphthongs in both medial and final positions. Furthermore, Garr specifically provides the example of *ym* as [*yom*] "day" (Yehimilk 5; Kilamu 12; Karatepe A I 5, etc.) as an example of diphthong contraction. In fact, Garr states: "Thus *\*aw* and *\*ay* contracted without exception throughout the Phoenician dialects."[49] Likewise, diphthong reductions of *aw* > *o* and *ay* > *e* are found to be complete in

---

[47] Garr 39.
[48] Sabatino Moscati, Anton Spitaler, Edward Ullendorff, and Wolfram von Soden, *An Introduction to the Comparative Grammar of the Semitic Languages*, ed. Sabatino Moscati (Wiesbaden: Otto Harrassowitz, 1980) 55.
[49] Garr 35.

Ugaritic as well as Tell Amarna glosses.[50] Thus, the attested *ym* would have been pronounced as *yom*. The example of parallel attestation of *ym* and *ywm* in Epigraphic South Arabian shows that the process of diphthong reduction was at an active stage.[51] Thus, this case also supports the fact that *ym* was pronounced as *yom*.

Garr's first explanation that *ym* represented one of the two existent early Biblical Hebrew singular form for "day," therefore, is not very convincing. Garr offers second explanation for the pervasive -- actually, exclusive[52] -- existence of the form *ym* for "day" in Southern Hebrew. Garr forwards that the form *ym* was, indeed, pronounced as *yom* as in Biblical Hebrew.

---

[50] Moscati *et al.* 54; Garr 35.

[51] Moscati *et al.* 55. Moscati *et al.* further mention that even though Classical Arabic fully preserves the original diphthong in its entirety, modern dialects of Arabic witness to extensive diphthong contraction (55). This points to the general tendency of diphthong to contraction in phonology, which has a bearing on orthography. Devens, therefore, states: "Spelling changes more slowly than does pronunciation and thus masks developments in the spoken language" (Monica S. Devens, "What Descriptive Phonologists Do: One Approach to the Study of Language, with Particular Attention to Biblical Hebrew," *Linguistics and Biblical Hebrew*, ed. Walter R. Bodine (Winona Lake: Eisenbrauns, 1992, pp. 7-16) 15).

[52] Garr finds it "surprising" that *ywm* "never appears" in Southern Hebrew texts (39).

But this form was borrowed from a diphthong-contracting dialect, probably from Northern Hebrew.[53]

The other exception of diphthong-contracted form in Southern Hebrew pointed out by Garr is *tld* (Tôlad) < *Tawlad, whose spelling Garr regards as surprising in light of the fact that the name belonged to a city in southern Judah. Garr believes that this is an example of defective reading, and the diphthong, therefore, should not have been read contracted.[54] Garr's conclusion regarding "defective reading" is based on his premise that diphthongs did not tend toward contraction in Judah. But taken at face value, this case supports the possibility of diphthong contraction in Judah.

These examples of *aw*-diphthong contraction parallels such diphthong contraction in the North and can be seen as characteristic of Southern Hebrew. Thus, the *waw* in '*wd* "still" (Shiloah 1:2; Arad 1:5, 2:7) and in *mws'* is *plene* writing of the contracted *ô* for the *aw*-diphthong.

When Garr makes the claim that Southern Hebrew diphthongs were uncontracted, Garr provides only the examples of '*wd* and *mws'* for the retention of *aw*-diphthongs.[55] Garr does not have a strong support for his claim. Even those, such as

---

[53] Garr 39.
[54] Garr 39.
[55] Garr 39.

Young, who claim the possibility of the general tendency in the South to diphthong retention point to *wd* and *mws'* as examples of diphthong reduction, although Young claims that they are dialectal characteristics accepted into Southern Hebrew.[56]

Other diphthongs that Garr claims were not contracted belong to the *ay*-diphthong group. The examples Garr provides are *byt*, "house" (Beer-sheba Ostraca 1:4; Silwan B 1; Mur 17 A 1) and *yyn*, "wine" (Arad 1:3, 9, etc.; Lach. 25).[57] Young agrees with Garr that these diphthongs were not contracted.[58] Yet, is it possible that these two *ay*-diphthong forms orthographically display *ay*-diphthong reduction into *ê* with a *mater lectionis*? In fact, even Young agrees with Barr in affirming that *matres lectionis* could be written or omitted after the diphthong reduction occurred. Young writes: "As Barr has pointed out, once the originally diphthongal *yod* and *waw* became *matres lectionis* they become optional. It was usual to write them, but a scribe could omit them just as he could omit any *matres lectionis*."[59]

In Northern Hebrew, there are clear examples of *ay*-diphthong reduction, such as *qês* "summer" (Gezer Calendar 7) and *yên*

---

[56] Young 199.
[57] Garr 39.
[58] Young 119.
[59] Young 167.

"wine" (Samaria Ostraca *passim*).⁶⁰ These were written without the *mater lectionis*; namely, the *yod*. In Northern Hebrew, however, a form with a *yod* in the medial position is attested; namely, $byt^{61}$ found in Tell Qasile 2.⁶²

Garr considers three possibilities for the form *byt*. Garr first considers that the *yod* may be a *mater lectionis*, but does not see this as very feasible because there are "no parallels to this usage." Second possibility according to Garr is that this form was borrowed from a dialect that did not contract diphthongs; Garr names Southern Hebrew as a possible source. Third possible explanation according to Garr is that since *byt* belongs to place names in both instances, it may reflect an earlier nonmonophthongizing dialect and not the current speech patterns.⁶³

Although Garr finally concludes that *byt* represents an uncontracted diphthong form,⁶⁴ the fact that Garr considered as one of the options the possibility that the *yod* was *mater lectionis* of [ê] is significant. Garr stated that there are no parallels, but *byt* in the construct form in Biblical Hebrew

---

⁶⁰ Garr 38.
⁶¹ Young claims that this form was not an example of diphthong contraction (167).
⁶² Garr 38.
⁶³ Garr 38-39.
⁶⁴ Garr 39.

evidences the *yod* as the *mater lectionis* of [ê].

*Plene* spelling of *yod* in originally *ay*-diphthong which has contracted to [ê] can be found in Aramaic in the Achaemenid Period (538-333 BC) as well. For instance, in the Hermopolis papyri written in Memphis, spelling both with and without *y* for the consonantal letter representing reduced *\*ay*-diphthong occur in *byt*, specifically, and in *\*qatl* formation, in general. The spelling without *y* occur once for noun *byt* in a construct form (HP 2, 12 [*bt*]) and once in a form with a pronominal suffix (HP 2, 15 [*bth*]). But in the same letter, *byt* of the construct form also occurs (HP 2, 1). There is a form *byty* (HP 1, 12) in which the first *y*, which would represent the reduced *ay*-diphthong, has been added above the line. This indicates that the scribe reviewing his letter corrected[65] the spelling representing the current pronunciation (*bty*) into the more historical spelling (*byty*).[66]

Another example from Aramaic in the Achaemenid period which attests to both exclusion and inclusion of *y* is *byn* in the

---

[65] This "correction" raises the question of the extent of scribal tendency to orthographic conservatism and its relation to phonetic developments and influence on orthographic conventions.

[66] M. L. Folmer, *The Aramaic Language in the Achaemenid Period: A Study in Linguistic Variation* (Leuven: Uitgeverij Peeters en Departement Oosterse Studies, 1995) 175.

legal documents from Elephantine. The preposition *byn* is originally a \**qatl* formation. *byn* with the third person plural masculine pronominal suffix occur without *y* in the writings of Nathan bar Ananiah (1) [*bnyhm*] and his son (3) [*bnyhm*]. These documents are dated to the second half of the fifth century BC.[67]

However, among contemporary documents, there is attestation of *byn* with the third person plural masculine pronominal suffix spelled with the historical *y* representing the reduced \**ay* diphthong. The form *bynyhm* is found in the legal documents written by Haggai bar Shemaiah (5) and in a document written by an unknown scribe in 420 BC (K 6) (2).[68]

Thus, Folmer concludes that there is evidence for the contraction of \**ay*-diphthong in the construct forms of *qatl* formations in Aramaic in the Achaemenid period, although Folmer sees "no evidence" in the Aramaic texts of the period for *ay*-diphthong contraction in absolute and emphatic forms[69] of *qatl*. But it is worthy to study the role of stress in the resistance to "diphthong con-

---

[67] Folmer 175.
[68] Folmer 176.
[69] It must be noted that Moscati *et al.* perceive exceptions in Egyptian Aramaic to diphthong reduction as purely orthographic in nature -- due to "instantces of historical spelling" (55), thus affirming general tendency to diphthong reduction.

traction" in absolute and emphatic forms.[70] Folmer acknowledges: "One may wonder to what extent stress has played in the contraction of this diphthong...."[71]

All in all, the case of Aramaic in the Achaemenid period shows instances of diphthong reduction which are written with *y*. Not only that, among the examples is the very form *byt*. Thus, Garr's assertion that *byt* written with *mater lectionis y* in Hebrew inscriptions does not have parallels[72] needs to be reassessed.

Furthermore, the forms *ynn* and *byt* in Southern Hebrew can function as parallel attestation of insertion of *yod* as *mater lectionis* of [ê]. In light of Barr's and Young's assertion that, to the scribe, the use of *matres lectionis* of originally diphthongal *yod* and *waw* was optional, it is not too difficult to see the possibility of the reduction of *ay*-diphthong to [ê].

---

[70] The question is further complicated in light of the fact that there is no general consensus concerning the origin of the official Aramaic of the Achaemenid period (Folmer 5). For, the disagreement provides difficulty for the study of diachronic development of Aramaic.
[71] Folmer 176.
[72] Although examination of diachronic development of Aramaic and its synchronic influence on Hebrew at various stages of Hebrew language history would have a bearing on the understanding of diphthong reduction in Hebrew, it would be too extensive of an enterprise for the present paper. Providing multiple attestation serves the purpose of the present work.

Thus, one sees general tendency in the Hebrew inscriptions to diphthong reduction. This is only one example of the commonality that the Hebrew inscriptions share with each other. Not only do Hebrew inscriptions find commonality among themselves, they share similarities with Biblical Hebrew. Thus, one cannot deny diachronic development of Hebrew before the exilic period.

When did Biblical Hebrew start? In light of the inscriptions, one can certainly state that Biblical Hebrew finds its origin in the pre-exilic period. Sáenz-Badillos believes that the Israelite tribes which settled in Canaan from the fourteenth to the thirteenth centuries BC used Hebrew as a spoken and written language until the fall of Jerusalem in 587 BC. Biblical Hebrew was the prestige literary language which existed alongside various dialects.[73] The function of literary prestige language of Biblical Hebrew in the midst of dialectal differences corresponding to diverse origins of Israel can be understood in light of the literary prestige language of Canaan found in Amarna letters.[74] In fact, Young asserts that the high language had an independent existence in the pre-Israelite period and was not a product of purification of the dialects of Israelite tribes. This explains why the

---

[73] Sáenz-Badillos 52.
[74] Young 17.

Hebrew dialects were not very similar to Biblical Hebrew at first.[75] Sáenz-Badillos affirms: "In any case, there is a clear continuity between Hebrew as it is historically attested and the language of the El-Amarna letters, which date from before the settlement of the Israelites in Canaan."[76]

The standardization of Hebrew occurred during the United Monarchy of David and Solomon. Young writes: "Standard Biblical Hebrew had its origin in the time of the United Monarchy.... A standard prose, which we termed 'Official Hebrew' was needed by the large centralized administration set up by David and Solomon to rule their empire."[77] Sáenz-Badillos also states: "Classical Hebrew prose is clearly linked to the reigns of David and Solomon and their successors in Jerusalem."[78]

One of the stylistic differences between Archaic Biblical Hebrew and Standard Biblical Hebrew is the strong Aramaic flavor of the former and the decrease of it in the latter. Indeed, the Deir Alla texts show us that just as Aramaic always had a Canaanizing tendency due to its common heritage with Canaanite,[79] Hebrew had the

---

[75] Young 80.
[76] Sáenz-Badillos 54.
[77] Young 97.
[78] Sáenz-Badillos 68.
[79] Moscati *et al.* argue that one cannot speak of a distinction between Canaanite and Aramaic before the first millennium BC, when Aramaic made its

tendency to be Aramaizing. Thus, the "Aramaic" influence existed long before the exile.[80] According to Young, it is no surprise in light of the hypothesis that Biblical Hebrew is merely a compromise prestige dialect of a people who had diverse dialects, which provided linguistic richness underneath the surface of Biblical Hebrew.[81] The standard Biblical Hebrew, as a nationalized form of an ancient Canaanite prestige language, enjoyed usage in the North as well as in the south, as is evidenced by Hosea and Amos in the North.[82]

Even the poets who wrote in Archaic Biblical Hebrew, whose end marks a significant stage in Biblical Hebrew, after which Standard Biblical Hebrew started, accepted a standard language, although archaic dialectal features appear more frequently in the literature of Archaic Biblical Hebrew. Thus, Young remarks: "The truth is, that the literary remains of ancient Hebrew are remarkably uniform."[83] In fact,

---

historic and epigraphic appearance, because in the second millennium BC, the isoglosses which distinguish the two groups had not yet been made. This does not preclude the variation in local speech-forms of the Northwest Semitic area, but this variety exhibits itself in forms different from those in the first millennium BC (7).

[80] Young 60.
[81] Young 18.
[82] Young 168.
[83] Young 17.

Archaic Biblical Hebrew finds such close proximity to Standard Biblical Hebrew, that Young states: "Basically we may see this as a change in style, rather than a linguistic development." [84] Sáenz-Badillos believes that this unity is not confined to ancient Hebrew, but, rather, extends to the whole of its history. Sáenz-Badillos states: "Nonetheless, from one perspective, especially if we concentrate on the written language, it is possible to speak of the historical unity of Hebrew throughout its existence. .... The truth of this statement even extends to the Hebrew spoken and written today, following a fascinating process of revival. The fundamental unity of Hebrew, both its language and its literature, is beyond doubt."[85]

---

[84] Young 20.
[85] Sáenz-Badillos 50.

## Works Cited

Devens, Monica S. "What Descriptive Phonologists Do: One Approach to the Study of Language, with Particular Attention to Biblical Hebrew." *Linguistics and Biblical Hebrew*. Ed. Walter R. Bodine. Winona Lake: Eisenbrauns, 1992, pp. 7-16.

Folmer, M. L. *The Aramaic Language in the Achaemenid Period: A Study in Linguistic Variation*. Leuven: Uitgeverij Peeters en Departement Oosterse Studies, 1995.

Garr, W. Randall. *Dialect Geography of Syria-Palestine, 1000-586 B.C.E.* Philadelphia: University of Pennsylvania Press, 1985.

Joüon, Paul, and T. Muraoka. *A Grammar of Biblical Hebrew*. Rome: Editrice Pontificio Istituto Biblico, 1993.

Kutscher, Eduard Yechezkel. *A History of the Hebrew Language*. Ed. Raphael Kutscher. Jerusalem: The Magnes Press (The Hebrew University), 1982.

Moscati, Sabatino, Anton Spitaler, Edward Ullendorff, and Wolfram von Soden. *An*

*Introduction to the Comparative Grammar of the Semitic Languages.* Ed. Sabatino Moscati. Wiesbaden: Otto Harrassowitz, 1980.

Rendsburg, Gary A. "Morphological Evidence for Regional Dialects in Ancient Hebrew." *Linguistics and Biblical Hebrew*. Ed. Walter R. Bodine. Winona Lake: Eisenbrauns, 1992, pp. 65-88.

Sáenz-Badillos, Angel. *A History of the Hebrew Language*. Tr. John Elwolde. Cambridge: Cambridge University Press, 1993.

Tigay, Jeffrey H. *You Shall Have No Other Gods: Israelite Religion in the Light of Hebrew Inscriptions*. Atlanta: Scholars Press, 1986.

Young, Ian. *Diversity in Pre-Exilic Hebrew*. Tübingen: J. C. B. Mohr (Paul Siebeck), 1993.

Zevit, Ziony. *Matres Lectionis in Ancient Hebrew Epigraphs*. Cambridge: American Schools of Oriental Research, 1980.

## The Making of Theodor Herz, the Father of the Jewish State of Israel[*]

Theodor Herzl unquestionably played a crucial role in the founding of a nation-home for the Jewish people. Herzl's contemporary and follower, Erwin Rosenberger, herald Herzl as "the Father of the modern Zionist movement."[1] And Herzl's biographer Israel Cohen credits Herzl with the creation of the State of Israel: "Without the First World War, there would have been no Balfour Declaration, without the Second, there would have been no State. And without the movement founded by Herzl, there would have been neither."[2]

How did Herzl come to play such an important role? A key to unlocking this question can be found in Herzl's identity. How did Herzl perceive himself? One

---

[*] I conducted my research on Theodor Herzl and Zionism under the guidance of Professor Ehud Sprinzak, the leading Israeli expert on Terrorism and modern Israeli politics in 1993-1994 when I lived in Jerusalem as a Raoul Wallenberg Scholar, investigating democracy and human rights.

[1] Erwin Rosenberger, *Herzl: As I Remember Him*, tr. Louis Jay Herman (New York: Herzl Press, 1959) 250.

[2] Israel Cohen, *Theodor Herzl: Founder of Political Zionism* (New York: Thomas Yoseloff, 1959) 369.

encounters some difficulty when one tries to decipher Herzl's self-perception. Conflicting evidence, such as Herzl's records at the University of Vienna, presents itself before the reader concerning how Herzl perceived his national identity and his position in the context of growing anti-Semitism. Indeed, Herzl struggled between German and Hungarian national identities since his youth, without his Jewish identity playing a significant role, originally, in his quest for a national identity. Herzl's conflict with nationalist identity clarifies itself in light of Herzl's experiences in his historical context and his parents' assimilationist educational philosophy.

In the context of nineteenth century Europe, in which national identity was very important for self-perception and individual identity, Theodor Herzl struggled and did not find satisfaction nor acceptance in either German or Hungarian national identity. This is understandable in light of the growing anti-Semitism that paralleled growing European nationalism's. Herzl came to realize the ephemeral nature of the "Jewish Emancipation" and embraced his Jewish identity as his national identity. With this realization, Herzl exerted himself to achieve the geographical-physical embodiment of his invisible national identity in the State of Israel in the Land of Israel.

In 1849, Jews received the right to live in all the cities of the Habsburg Empire, such as Pest and Vienna. Thus, many Jews moved from their little towns and villages to major cities. Such measure of "emancipation" was brought to Europe as the result of Magyar nationalist revolts in the years 1848-1849, against the Habsburg Austrian rulers, led by the Hungarian national hero, Kossuth Lajos (1802-1894), a son of a Slovak father and a German mother.[3] For Hungary, nationalist struggles resulted in Emperor Franz Joseph granting *Ausgleich*, formal equal status, of Hungary to Austria within the Empire in 1867. Empress Elisabeth became the Queen of Hungary.[4] Magyar nationalism, therefore, saw fruit.

In the context of this "emancipation" of Jews and burgeoning nationalism, Herzl, born in Hungary in 1860, struggled with his identity, especially his national identity. Herzl wavered between Hungarian and German national identities. This is nowhere more poignant than in his identification of his mother tongue at the law faculty of the University of Vienna. As attested in his university records, he indicated his mother tongue as German in the first semester in 1878, but stated Hungarian as his mother

---

[3] Avner Falk, *Herzl, King of the Jews: A Psychoanalytic Biography of Theodor Herzl* (Lanham: University Press of America, 1993) 4.
[4] Falk 19.

tongue in the next semester. Hungarian remained his mother tongue on the university records until the summer semester of 1881, when Herzl again stated German as the mother tongue.[5] It is true that he grew up speaking both German and Hungarian. But his birthplace was Pest, a Hungarian city. Why did he even consider German as his mother tongue?

One can understand Herzl's consideration of himself as German, or relating to German national identity, in the historical context of rising German nationalism, which was pervasive in Vienna, the city to which Herzl's family moved from Hungary when Herzl was eighteen years old. Herzl wanted to be a part of the triumphant, the powerful. This is evidenced in his joining the student dueling fraternity, *Wiener academische Burschenschaft Albia*, which was part of the growing German nationalism, despite the fact that there was a parallel anti-Semitism, which was a part of German nationalism.[6]

Herzl's biographers have sought to understand this behavior. Falk perceives this action as a picture into Herzl's masochism, characteristic of a narcissistic personality. Falk writes: "This was a masochistic and self-defeating act. The Jew-hating *Albia* was bound to reject him eventually, when

---

[5] Steven Beller, *Herzl* (London: Peter Halban Publishers Ltd., 1991) 4.
[6] Beller 5-6.

the Jewish Question came up."[7] Beller, on the other hand, does not see Herzl as a masochist who openly entered a situation fraught with inevitable rejection and hatred. Beller argues that Herzl perceived the anti-Semitism attached to German nationalism as "cultural" anti-Semitism, which rejected Jews who did not assimilate into the German culture. Beller writes: "Nevertheless, a young Jew such as Herzl could see this anti-Semitism as not so much a rejection of himself, as of those money-grabbing, un-cultured Jews who had not integrated themselves properly into German culture."[8] Herzl, perceiving himself as culturally assimilated, believed that he could be a part of the growing German nationalism. Falk agrees with Beller in the essential concept that Herzl wanted to be "German." Falk writes that, in *Albia*, Herzl "...attempted to be more German than the Germans in it."[9]

Herzl's efforts to make German national identity his own can be further understood in light of his desire to survive and succeed in Vienna, his New World, and to leave his Old World behind. Falk states: "Herzl's infatuation with Vienna and his frivolous adoption of the name *Theodor Viennensis* concealed his growing estrangement from and contempt for his native

---

[7] Falk 70.
[8] Beller 5.
[9] Falk 179.

Hungary."[10] Falk describes Herzl's reference to Vienna, his New World, as "infatuation," and his relation to Hungary, the Old World, with the words, "estrangement" and "contempt."

However, other scholars, who agree with Falk's point concerning Herzl's desire to succeed in Vienna, do not place Vienna and Hungary in such antipodal positions in reference to Herzl. One such scholar is Andrew Handler. Handler describes Herzl's seeming disdain for Hungary as a "passing phase," as a result of patriotism that immigrants exhibit in order to succeed in the New World. Handler argues: "Thus his arrogant remarks, far from reflecting an immutable perspective, are more representative of a passing phase -- the sudden upsurge of patriotism that many immigrants display toward their new country to the detriment of the one that they left, in an effort to prove the sincerity and success of assimilation to themselves and others they hope to impress."[11] Thus, Herzl's perceived importance of German national identity for success in Vienna explains Herzl's efforts to embrace it.

But, was it possible for Herzl to leave behind eighteen years of life and per-

---

[10] Falk 71.
[11] Andrew Handler, *Dori: The Life and Times of Theodor Herzl in Budapest (1860-1878)* (Alabama: The University of Alabama Press, 1983) 3.

sonal experiences in Hungary? He was not able to, as evident in his stating Hungarian as his mother tongue for many years at the University of Vienna after he had originally stated German as his mother tongue. After all, Herzl was a product of Hungarian national identity, which was prevalent in Pest during his childhood as the result of the Kossuth Lajos's revolts. Thus, Handler is convinced that Herzl's childhood "was also deeply affected by the sights and sounds of his environment. Herzl Tivadar, nicknamed Dori, was in every way as much a Magyar boy in Budapest as Theodor Herzl would be an assimilated Austrian in Vienna."[12] The "Magyar boy" identity did not merely disappear in Vienna. That partly explains Herzl's struggle with national identity and his perception of his own "mother tongue."

Indeed, Herzl's relationship to Hungary was significant for him and remained so. Handler forwards: "Herzl never truly left Budapest, physically or emotionally."[13] This is more than understandable in light of his deeply personal experiences in Hungary. For instance, his beloved sister Pauline, whom Falk regards as the "single most important person in Theodor's emotional life after his mother,"[14] died in Hungary and was buried there. Although Falk's insinu-

---

[12] Handler 25.
[13] Handler 3.
[14] Falk 18.

ation of Herzl's incestuous feeling for Pauline lacks substantial source support,[15] his recognition of Pauline's personal importance to Herzl should not be minimized. For, despite the fact that Herzl and his parents moved permanently to Vienna in 1878, after the death of his sister Pauline, Herzl visited her grave in Budapest every anniversary of her death until he met his own death.[16]

Furthermore, Hungary was personally significant in Herzl's romantic life. Herzl's first love experience was in Pest in the summer of 1875. During that summer, the fifteen-year-old Herzl fell in love with Madeleine Kurz, who was fourteen or fifteen at the time. He wrote an eight-line poetry with her name, "Madeleine," as the title.[17] Herzl's first love Madeleine died in her teens, like Pauline.[18] This first love in Hungary made a deep impression on Herzl; for, years later after he had left Hungary

---

[15] Falk 18-19. Only source support that Falk provides for his argument for Herzl's incestuous feeling for his sister is the autobiographical sketch in which Herzl had fought Pauline and then "sealed her mouth with a brotherly kiss to make up after a mock quarrel." In this unpublished autobiographical sketch, Herzl himself used the word "brotherly" to describe the nature of the kiss, which, on its face value, points to the harmless nature of the sign of reconciliation.
[16] Handler 3.
[17] Falk 39.
[18] Falk 42.

Herzl fell in love with Madeleine Kurz's niece. Herzl was twenty-five years old and Magda Fuchs was only thirteen years old. Herzl, however, found himself love-sick and poured out his feeling of amorous agony onto his diary on January 10, 1886, a day after he fell in love with Madeleine's niece Magda.[19] But Herzl's love was not reciprocated.

About a month later, on February 28, 1886, the love-sick Herzl met and fell in love with Julie Naschauer.[20] This love, which was consummated in marriage, further shows that Herzl's heart was in Hungary; for, Julie moved to Vienna in 1880, as a second-generation Hungarian, who had lived in Pest, the city of Herzl's birth and youth. Thus, Handler argues that Herzl's Hungarian national identity was one of the significant factors that contributed to Herzl's emotional composition even in Vienna, his New World. Handler states: "His burgeoning romantic interests were, to be sure, played out in a Viennese setting, but the emotional roots of his love for Julie Naschauer, his future wife, were firmly planted in a background of common social standing, religion, and national origin."[21] Hungarian national origin was a factor that

---

[19] Falk 101.
[20] Falk 103-104.
[21] Handler 3.

played a crucial role in Herzl's identity as a person and in the way he related to others. Indeed, among Herzl's close friends were individuals of Hungarian descent; Max Nordau was one such individual. In 1895, Nordau was one of the first individuals who readily espoused Herzl's ideas found in *The Jewish State*, and Nordau encouraged Herzl to pursue his ideas,[22] at a time when many not only rejected Herzl's ideas but also considered him crazy. One such individual was Herzl's friend, Fredrich Schiff, who urged Herzl to seek medical help, after hearing Herzl's ideas found in *The Jewish State* in their earlier form in the *Rothschild Address*. Schiff was so concerned that he came again the next day and pressed Herzl to abandon his ideas and seek the counsel of Max Nordau, with the expectation that Nordau would also discourage Herzl.[23] But, Nordau, as mentioned, championed Herzl's cause.

This Max Nordau and Herzl were both born and raised in Pest. Herzl left with his family at the age eighteen, and Nordau moved to Paris at the age of thirty-one. There were occasional outbursts and tension in their friendship, but they had a special bond, of which Herzl was conscious. This

---

[22] Alex Bein, *Theodor Herzl: A Biography*, tr. Maurice Samuel (Philadelphia: The Jewish Publication Society of America, 1962) 156-157.
[23] Bein 140-141.

friendship increased Herzl's contact with other Hungarians.²⁴

Not only was Hungary significant in his personal, emotional life, it was professionally significant for Herzl. Herzl had his literary start in Pest, when he founded the literary society, *Wir*, early in 1874, in his last year at the *Realschule*, which he had entered in 1870. The *Realschule* was a seconddary school that emphasized the sciences and modern languages at the expense of a classical training in Greek and Latin. Herzl was not interested in the subjects that would make him an engineer, so he did poorly in them. His affinity to literature drove him to spend much time with *Wir*, which in turn did not help his school grades, but which did expand Herzl's literary horizon.²⁵

Despite the fact that Herzl's "baby" *Wir* found its birth and presence in Hungary, many of Herzl's biographers emphasize Herzl's adoration of the German language and affinity to German nationalism even when Herzl was a youth in Hungary. One such biographer is Amos Elon, who devotes a whole chapter, entitled "German Boy in Budapest."²⁶ Elon argues that Herzl adopted

---

²⁴ Handler 4.
²⁵ Desmond Stewart, *Theodor Herzl: Artist and Politician* (London: Hamish Hamilton, 1974) 37-41.
²⁶ Amos Elon, *Herzl* (New York: Holt, Rinehart and Winston, 1975) 11-31 (chapter two).

German national identity for himself and admitted that, if he had the choice, he would have preferred to be born a Prussian nobleman.[27] According to Elon, German national identity was a natural part of Herzl. Elon states: "There was something natural and obvious in young Herzl's support of German nationalism and grandeur."[28] In order to support the thesis that German nationalism was the most significant element in Herzl's self identity as a young individual in Pest, Elon points to Herzl's historical poem, entitled "To Canossa We Won't Go," which Herzl composed in the wake of the Prussian victory over France in 1870. Since the poem represents a significant element in Elon's argument for Herzl's German national identity in Hungary, it is quoted here from Elon's book:

> Out of the long, long night
> Through Luther's power and might
> The German spirit came to light.
>
> And Liberty's glorious sight
> Shines upon all awake; for lo,
> To Canossa we won't go!
>
> (Es ist aus langer Nacht
> Durch Luther's gewaltige Kraft
> Der deutsche Geist erwacht.

---

[27] Elon 15.
[28] Elon 25.

Und der Freiheit goldnes Licht
Bestrahlt der Erwachenden Angesicht
Nach Canossa gehn wir nicht.)²⁹

Herzl wrote this poem in German to express his German nationalist sentiment. But it is one thing to argue that Herzl possessed an affinity to German nationalism alongside his Hungarian nationalism, but it is quite an another thing to call Herzl a "German boy in Budapest."

Indeed, not all scholars agree with Elon's thesis that German nationalist identity was Herzl's pervasive identity or that Herzl preferred and used the German language predominantly for his literary and personal expression in his youth in Pest. Beller notes, defiantly: "The teenage Herzl was as good a writer in Hungarian as he was in German."³⁰ And competence in a language requires constant usage and refinement. Therefore, Handler argues that the stereotype of Herzl's affinity to the German language and, by extension, to German national identity is based on isolated source materials familiar to Herzl's biographers. Handler states: "The German compositions are also the ones that have since become familiar to Herzl's biographers. But it is a mistake to suppose that the best-known

---

²⁹ Elon 25.
³⁰ Beller 3.

sources are the only ones."[31] Handler states that Herzl most likely read the compositions that he wrote in Magyar for his school at the meetings of his literary society. However, many of these Hungarian compositions, which would support the thesis of Herzl's affinity to the Hungarian language and Hungarian national identity, are, unfortunately, largely unknown to us at the present.[32] But enough of Herzl's early compositions in Hungarian exist[33] to affirm Herzl's awareness of Hungarian nationalism and his proclivity to it. Handler writes: "Herzl spoke Hungarian flawlessly and wrote in that language with unusual flair and imagination. His earliest compositions, many of which I had occasion to examine at the Central Zionist Archives in Jerusalem, reveal great enthusiasm for and profound understanding of Hungarian nationalism, its literary bases, and its political objectives."[34]

Therefore, scholars, such as Handler, warn against perceiving Herzl's occasional critical remarks on things Hungarian and Herzl's decision to pursue a literary career in German as evidences for Herzl's per-

---

[31] Handler 61.
[32] Handler 61.
[33] Helpful insight into Herzl's Hungarian compositions can be found in Joseph Patai's essay, "Herzl's School Years, " found in *Herzl Year Book (Volume 3): Herzl Centennial Issue*, ed. Raphael Patai (New York: Herzl Press, 1960, pp. 53-75).
[34] Handler xii.

vasive German national identity and contempt for Hungarian identity. Handler states: "The myth is the result of overestimating the importance of isolated statements rather than considering the merits of circumstance and documentary evidence." [35] Indeed, Herzl's emotional and professional experience in Hungary, as well as his youth in Pest in the midst of Hungarian nationalism, does not support the thesis of exclusive German national identity and absence of Hungarian national identity. Handler poetically encapsulates the impact of Hungary on Herzl: "The sounds and sights of Budapest had not been dimmed by either distance or time. Nor could the experience of eighteen years have faded so completely or have been so consciously suppressed as not to have left a substantial residue."[36] It was, indeed, the real presence of Hungarian identity that contributed partly to Herzl's conflict with his German national identity.

Herzl's family environment did not help to minimize his struggle with national identity. Herzl's parents did not encourage Herzl's Jewish identity. They were among those who supported the idea of assimilation as a means to achieve acceptance into the surrounding national identity. Adler writes: "The supporters of assimilation were con-

---
[35] Handler 95.
[36] Handler 118.

vinced that the Jews would eventually become an organic part of the peoples among whom they lived. Assimilation, they reasoned, would eliminate the cause of anti-Semitism. Herzl had been reared in a family that believed in assimilation, and he had great difficulty trying to shed its effects."[37] The evidence of the effects of assimilationist ideas on Herzl's psyche can be found in the fact that Herzl did not circumcise his son, Hans, who was born in the summer of 1891.[38] Hans did undergo circumcision, but much later, at the age of fifteen, two years more than the age for Bar Mitzvah.[39] Herzl did not fulfill his duty as a Jewish parent, to affirm his son's inclusion in the covenant, important in the Jewish concept of the chosen people of God.

In social terms, Herzl did not affirm Hans' Jewish identity; for, circumcision is an important sign of Jewishness (and a public Jewish ceremony) as attested in Jewish religious texts in which circumcision is heralded as the sign of the covenant between God and his people, affirming every circumcised male member as a member of the chosen nation. Herzl did not encourage Hans' active participation in Jewish

---

[37] Joseph Adler, *The Herzl Paradox: Political, Social and Economic Theories of a Realist* (New York: Hadrian Press, 1962) 68.
[38] Beller 12.
[39] Beller 124.

life and community. Herzl's struggle with his nationalist identity, exacerbated by his parents' assimilationist family education, explains his actions at the time of Hans' birth andin his child-rearing philosophy.

Herzl's childhood experience, under assimilationist ideas, was not an isolated one. Many of Herzl's contemporaneous Jewish youths, also, experienced dearth of opportunities for exploration of their Jewish identity. Mahrer writes: "Herzl's whole childhood and youth had as little contact with Judaism and Jewish problems as had the whole Jewish middle class of Central and Western Europe in that period. Nevertheless, the very position of Western European Jewry between the bonds of Jewish tradition and the lure of assimilation, was charged with more psychological conflict than that of the Eastern European Jew."[40] Indeed, it was the non-encouragement of Herzl's Jewish identity that created uncertainty of Herzl's self-perception and nationalist identity.

Not only did Herzl's parents not encourage Herzl's Jewish identity, they further added to his identity crisis by presenting two separate nationalist identities. German and Hungarian identities found

---

[40] Grete Mahrer, "Herzl's Return to Judaism," *Herzl Year Book (Volume 2): Essays in Zionist History and Thought*, ed. Raphael Patai (New York: Herzl Press, 1959, pp. 28-55) 29.

conflicting existence at Herzl's home. One example of this is found in the two names that Herzl's parents gave to Herzl, when he was born on May 2, 1860: a Hungarian one, Hercl Tivadar, and a German one, Theodor Herzl. Furthermore, Herzl's father Jacob, preferred to communicate with him in Magyar, or Hungarian, whereas his mother, Jeanette, preferred and used German as the language of communication with her son.[41] Falk describes the impact that such conflict in identity had on Herzl in psychological terms: "This double-language and double-name setup may have reinforced the process of ego splitting that went on inside him; he was like two people rolled into one."[42] Herzl stating German and Hungarian as his mother tongue at the University of Vienna records is the result of his conflict with national identity from his youth in Hungary, with parents who added to the confusion.

Herzl, however, did not find satisfaction in either of the two national identities; that is why he struggled between German and Hungarian nationalisms. In the midst of rising anti-Semitism even against most integrated Jews, like Alfred Dreyfus,[43]

---

[41] Falk 19.
[42] Falk 24.
[43] On December 27, 1894, Herzl wrote that Dreyfus had told the non-commissioned officer on guard that he was the victim of a personal vendetta and that he was being persecuted because he was a Jew. Alex Bein doubts that Dreyfus, as an assimilated Jew,

Herzl [44] came to realize that his national identity could only be found in his Jewish identity.

Herzl's diary entry entitled, "Begun in Paris around Pentecost 1895," provides a good example of this realization. The entry provides information regarding Herzl's

---

actually said that, but Bein points out that this report is significant in understanding Herzl's mind, as it was the first time that Herzl mentioned the Jewishness of Dreyfus in his articles on the Dreyfus affair, whose actual trial began on December 19, 1894 (Bein 111-112).

[44] Herzl had, personally, experienced rising anti-Semitism in his university in Vienna as a member of the dueling fraternity, *Albia*. Members were audibly expressing their support of Schoener and his anti-Semitic political speeches. Furthermore, in 1882, a Pan-Germanic, anti-Semitic student organization, *Der Verein deutscher Studenten in Wien*, was founded. On March 5, 1883, this organization arranged a memorial ceremony for Richard Wagner, and a member of *Albia*, Hermann Bahr, addressed the crowd and spoke favorably of "Wagnerian anti-Semitism." When Bahr declared himself a convert to the Pan-Germanic, anti-Semitic movement, he was received with enthusiasm by the crowd. Although Herzl did not attend the memorial meeting, he wrote a letter two days later, condemning *Albia*'s association with the meeting, and strongly urged the fraternity to disavow association from the anti-Semitic movement. Herzl tendered his resignation to *Albia*. After some debate on not accepting the resignation, but rather expelling Herzl from the fraternity, *Albia* sent a few lines of note to Herzl on April 3, 1883, that Herzl's name was removed and that Herzl should hand in his fraternity insignia (Bein 39-42).

personal experience with anti-Semitism, his description of it, and his response to it. The entry records that, two times, Herzl heard anti-Semitic slurs thrown at him. Herzl describes in his diary:

> Up till now I have heard with my own ears the cry of "Hep, Hep!" only twice. The first time was when I was passing through Mainz, in 1888. One evening I entered a cheap cabaret and drank my beer. As I was leaving and pushing my way out through the noise and bustle to the door, a fellow called "Hep, Hep!" after me. Around him rose a chorus of guffaws. The second time was at Baden near Vienna. As I drove in a carriage out of Hinterbrühl, from Speidel's home, someone shouted "Saujud!" at me. The cry struck deeper because it came as the fitting sequel to my conversation in Hinterbrühl, and it resounded on my "home" soil.[45]

---

[45] Marvin Lowenthal (ed. and tr.), *The Diaries of Theodor Herzl* (New York: The Dial Press, 1956) 6.

Both times, anti-Semitic epithets were thrown at Herzl by strangers who did not know Herzl. They were not concerned with the extent of his assimilation; they isolated him socially from themselves because he was a Jew. Herzl's entry above shows his self-realization that he did not belong in the "in-group." In describing the first incident, Herzl notes a "chorus of guffaws" that followed the anti-Semitic title. From Herzl's description, one can see that the anti-Semitic cry was loud, for Herzl was exiting the pub in the midst of a loud atmosphere that is so characteristic of pubs in general, and enough people paid attention to the comment and responded with mocking laughter.

The second anti-Semitic cry was thrown also by a stranger, who did not care whether Herzl was an assimilated Jew or not; to the anti-Semite, Herzl was a "pig-Jew." Herzl points out that he was hurt by the second incident more than the first because it happened at "home," near Vienna, the New World where he had wanted to find acceptance. Furthermore, it happened after his conversation with Ludwig Speidel regarding anti-Semitism.

It is important to note that Herzl understood the incident as an example of anti-Semitism, directed against Jews as a group. Herzl describes his reaction:

> I was enraged. I turned around bitterly in the direction of the two youngsters, but they were already far behind. In no time, too, my impulse to scuffle with street lads had vanished. Moreover, there had been no personal affront, for I was unknown to them: the insult was directed to my Jewish nose and beard, which they had glimpsed in the semidarkness behind the cab lanterns.[46]

Herzl felt that his Jewishness, which Herzl described in physical terms, prevented his acceptance by his countrymen at his own "home."

The incident reinforced Herzl's perception of anti-Semitism, which he had expounded to Speidel moments before the experience. Herzl described Jews as a group foreign to the land that they inhabit. Herzl told Speidel: "I understand what anti-Semitism is about. We Jews have maintained ourselves, even if through no fault of our own, as a foreign body among the different

---

[46] Herzl's diary, "Begun in Paris around Pentecost 1895," found in Lowenthal 10.

nations."[47] Herzl believed that the Jews as a group did not find identity in any European nation; they were a distinct group, "a foreign body." This comment of Herzl shows that Herzl realized his identity in terms of Jewish nationalist identity. Herzl did not belong to his childhood Hungary nor to his "home" Austria; his identity was with the Jewish people – the Jewish nation.

The surface appearance of integration and the legality of emancipation seemed all fleeting to Herzl. Herzl writes concerning the condition of the Jews of his time: "Their equality before the law, granted by statute, has become practically a dead letter. They are debarred from filling even moderately high positions, either in the army, or in any public or private capacity. And attempts are made to thrust them out of business also: 'Don't buy of Jews!'"[48] Legal equality did not mean destruction of anti-Semitism or the expression of that.

In fact, Herzl attributes the increase in anti-Semitism partly to legal emancipation itself. Herzl argues that, in the spirit of emancipation, equal right for Jews before the law was granted, and, since it has been conceded, it cannot be taken back. There-

---

[47] Herzl's diary, "Begun in Paris around Pentecost 1895," found in Lowenthal 9.
[48] Theodor Herzl, *The Jewish State*, tr. Sylvie d'Avigdor (London: Central Office of the Zionist Organization, 1934) 22.

fore, legal means to hurt Jews having become inaccessible, anti-Semitism and social expression of that grew more and more. Herzl encapsulates: "The very impossibility of getting at the Jews nourishes and embitters hatred of them. Anti-Semitism increases day by day and hour by hour among the nations; indeed, it is bound to increase, because the causes of its growth continue to exist and cannot be removed."[49] According to Herzl, the cause of anti-Semitism can be traced back to the Middle Ages, and its waste cannot but pass down. Herzl writes: "It is a remnant of the Middle Ages, which civilized nations do not even yet seem to shake off, try as they will."[50] Therefore, Herzl concludes: "Wherever they [Jews] live in perceptible numbers, they are more or less persecuted."[51] Herzl, therefore, believed that anti-Semitism would continue, except in a nation of Jews.

Furthermore, assimilation is not the answer, because assimilationist efforts will go unaccepted by the people, whose nationalist identity would bar those assimilationist attempts. Herzl acknowledges: "We might perhaps be able to merge ourselves entirely into surrounding races, if these were to leave us in peace. For a little period they manage to tolerate us, and then

---

[49] Herzl, *The Jewish State* 26.
[50] Herzl, *The Jewish State* 14.
[51] Herzl, *The Jewish State* 22.

their hostility breaks out again and again."[52] Herzl was talking from experience. Herzl had struggled with two nationalist identities -- namely, German and Hungarian -- since his childhood in a home that encouraged assimilation. Herzl did not find satisfaction or acceptance. Thus, Herzl came to realize that his nationalist identity was found in his Jewish identity. Herzl proclaims: "We are a people -- one people."[53] Jewish identity cannot be merged or subsumed because it is a national identity.

For Herzl, Jewish national identity came to be the most satisfactory national identity; therefore, Herzl wanted to see the fruition of the geographical-political embodiment of the State of Israel, as a physical reality to his inner realization and invisible identity. Herzl realized the importance of physical, visible embodiment of invisible reality. And an example of this can be found in his letter to Baron de Hirsch, in which Herzl expounded on the power of a flag. Herzl writes: "With a flag you can lead men where you will -- even into the Promised Land. Men live and die for a flag; it is indeed the only thing for which they are willing to die in masses...."[54] A flag is a physical embodiment of a national identity,

---

[52] Herzl, *The Jewish State* 27.
[53] Herzl, *The Jewish State* 15.
[54] Herzl's diary, "Whit Monday, June 3, 1895," found in Lowenthal 22.

which was an important element in self-perception and individual identity in Herzl's time. Herzl believed that national identity was important enough that masses will give their life for a symbol of that identity; namely, the flag. The value of a flag points to the real value of a geographical-political embodiment of the nationhood that the flag represents or would represent.

Herzl's perception of himself as a member of the Jewish nation, and the perceived importance of this identity for Herzl personally drove him for the cause of Zionism -- for the realization of the geographical-political embodiment of his identity. For Herzl, this physical reality was especially important. Herzl had struggled with two different national identities that really had no hope for future in his mind. Herzl's perception of himself required an essential element of nationhood; he was an intellectual product of his age, which made national identity as an important element of personal identity. In Herzl's opinion, his worth depended on the realization of a physical Jewish nation. Thus, Herzl was personally engaged in and worked for Zionism to the point of death, so to speak.

Herzl's efforts to find his own national identity corresponded to the need of other Jews of his time, who were also looking for a national identity. At a time of European nationalisms, many Jews, like

Herzl, came to realize that even the most assimilated of them were not included in the nationalist identities of Europe; their Jewish identity prevented that. Herzl's vision and personal need for a geographical-political embodiment of Jewish national identity, therefore, found followers among fellow Jews, who shared Herzl's conflicts and needs, in regards to identity.[55] Falk writes: "Herzl may have seemed a dreamer to many Jews; others were more receptive to his ideas, because of their own needs. His fantasies derived from overwhelmingly inner personal conflicts. They happened to respond to the real plight of the Jews in antisemitic Europe."[56]

---

[55] Herzl's followers who put so much trust in him and his vision for a Jewish state further propelled Herzl in his efforts. Herzl writes in his diary entry, "Folkstone, July 15, [1896]": "And while I was listening, on that people's tribune, to the fulsome words and the cheering of my adherents, I made a firm and silent resolve to become ever worthier of their trust and love" (found in Lowenthal 182-183).
[56] Falk 218.

## Works Cited and Consulted

Adler, Joseph. *The Herzl Paradox: Political, Social and Economic Theories of a Realist.* New York: Hadrian Press, 1962.

Bein, Alex. *Theodor Herzl: A Biography.* Tr. Maurice Samuel. Philadelphia: The Jewish Publication Society of America, 1962.

Beller, Steven. *Herzl.* London: Peter Halban Publishers Ltd., 1991.

Cohen, Israel. *Theodor Herzl: Founder of Political Zionism.* New York: Thomas Yoseloff, 1959.

Dethloff, Klaus. *Theodor Herzl oder Der Moses des Fin de siècle.* Wien: Hermann Böhlaus Nachf., 1986.

Elon, Amos. *Herzl.* New York: Holt, Rinehart and Winston, 1975.

Falk, Avner. *Herzl, King of the Jews: A Psychoanalytic Biography of Theodor Herzl.* Lanham: University Press of America, 1993.

Handler, Andrew. *Dori: The Life and Times of Theodor Herzl in Budapest (1860-1878)*. Alabama: The University of Alabama Press, 1983.

Herzl, Theodor. *The Jewish State*. Tr. Sylvie d'Avigdor. London: Central Office of the Zionist Organization, 1934.

Herzl, Theodor. *Zionist Writings: Essays and Addresses (Volume 1: January, 1896 - June, 1898)*. Tr. Harry Zohn. New York: Herzl Press, 1973.

Lewisohn, Ludwig. *Theodor Herzl: A Portrait for this Age*. Cleveland: The World Publishing Company, 1955.

Lowenthal, Marvin (Ed. and Tr.). *The Diaries of Theodor Herzl*. New York: The Dial Press, 1956.

O'Brien, Conor Cruise. *The Siege: The Saga of Israel and Zionism*. New York: Simon & Schuster, 1986.

Patai, Raphael (Ed.). *Herzl Year Book (Volume 2): Essays in Zionist History and Thought*. New York: Herzl Press, 1959.

Patai, Raphael (Ed.). *Herzl Year Book (Volume 3): Herzl Centennial Issue.* New York: Herzl Press, 1960.

Patai, Raphael (Ed.). *The Complete Diaries of Theodor Herzl (Volume 1).* Tr. Harry Zohn. New York: Herzl Press, 1960.

Rosenberger, Erwin. *Herzl: As I Remember Him.* Tr. Louis Jay Herman. New York: Herzl Press, 1959.

Stewart, Desmond. *Theodor Herzl: Artist and Politician.* London: Hamish Hamilton, 1974.

**Heerak Christian Kim**

# The Primacy of Immediate Small Group Identity: A Criticism of Recent Nationalistic Interpretations of the First Century[*]

Europe has been deeply impacted by nationalistic movements of the nineteenth century. In many ways nineteenth century nationalistic movements in Europe fundamentally changed the way Europeans viewed themselves, their society, their leaders, and the world around them. These nationalism movements also impacted the academic world and have left a lasting mark. In this paper, I would like to analyze one strand of European nationalism and to show that its impact on scholarship should be seen with a more critical eye. The nineteenth century European nationalism which I would like to examine is Zionism.

Zionism has impacted the study of early Christianity in profound ways and so

---

[*] This paper was delivered at the Critical Theory and Biblical Interpretation section of the International Society of Biblical Literature conference held during the month of July, 2004, in Groningen, the Netherlands. This paper represents my on-going critical thinking and research into formulating a framework methodology for examining early Christianity and ancient Judaism.

far there has not been much critical thinking on its impact. I would like argue that Zionist influences propelled New Testament studies towards a nationalist approach that denigrated more immediate and more real group and individual identities. The result is a skewed picture of the first century and an inaccurate understanding of early Christianity. I will particularly examine two leading figures who represent such a medium of Zionism in studying early Christianity; namely, Solomon Schlechter and Geza Vermes.

Solomon Schlechter is a giant in the study of the late Second Temple period and Rabbinic Judaism. After having won the patronage of Claude Montifiore, a member of a prominent Jewish noble family in England in the mid-nineteenth century, Solomon Schlechter was brought to the United Kingdom to push his vision for studying the Late Antiquity of Israel.[1] Although he did not formally declare his overt allegiance until 1906, Schlechter pushed a type of Zionist *Weltanshauung* for the study of Late Antiquity far before his public declaration for Zionism.[2] Schlechter's Zionist vision and

---

[1] Norman Bentwich (ed.), *Selected Writings: Solomon Schlechter* (Oxford: East and West Library, 1946), pp. 11-12.

[2] Bentwich, *Selected Writings: Solomon Schlecter*, p. 18.

interpretation is encapsulated in the phrase, "Catholic Israel."

For some, the term itself may be puzzling. Schlechter was adamant about stripping Judaism of any Christian interpretation and took an active anti-Christian stance. Solomon Schlechter describes an ideal Jewish commentary on the Bible in this way: "A Jewish commentary will also be free from such blasphemies as Jehveolatry, the 'whimsical God of Israel,' and similar offensive terms. And above all it must teach us that we are the fulfilment of the Word of God, and that the Old Testament and the whole history of Israel are not a mere preamble to the history of Christianity."[3] Yet, Schlechter decided to use the term "catholic" to describe Jewish national identity.

When one examines why Schlechter chose to use the term "catholic," his choice becomes understandable. Schlechter understood in "Catholic Israel" a vibrant Jewish community whose identity was in participation. Schlechter, in fact, used sacramental-type language to describe this participation and identity. Schlechter writes: "The norm as well as the sanction of Judaism is the practice actually in vogue. Its consecration is the consecration of general

---

[3] S. Schlechter, *Seminary Addresses and Other Papers* (Cincinnati: ARK Publishing Co., 1915), p. 5.

use – or, in other words, of Catholic Israel. It was probably with a view to this communion that the later mystics introduced a short prayer to be said before the performance of any religious ceremony, in which, among other things, the speaker professes his readiness to act in the name of all Israel."[4]

Distinctive Christian language used by Solomon Schlechter indicates the extent to which he was influenced by Christian discourse. As much as Schlechter consciously attacked Christian influences on Judaism, he could not free himself from his context and the cultural language setting in which he found himself. It was only through the prevailing discourse he was able to express himself and make himself understood to English speaking Jews.

In the same way that Schlechter is a product of the Christian culture in which he found himself and utilized its discourse to advance his ideas in Judaism, Schlechter was very much a product of the nineteenth century European nationalism. It was in this context and language setting that Schlechter expressed himself and described Judaism. But unlike Christian cultural influences which in principle Schlechter opposed, he embraced nineteenth century European nationalism wholeheartedly – but with Jewish

---

[4] Bentwich, *Selected Writings: Solomon Schlechter*, pp. 36-37.

content. However, for Schlechter Jewish nationalism was necessarily religious. Schlechter writes: "The rebirth of Israel's national consciousness, and the revival of Israel's religions, or, to use a shorter term, the revival of Judaism, are inseparable. When Israel lost itself, or began to work at self-effacement, it was sure to deny its God."[5] For Schlechter, "Catholic Israel" served the emphasis of uniting nineteenth century Jewish nationalism with the Jewish religion.

Schlechter's nationalist emphasis was not confined to his *Weltanschauung* for society and politics. Schlechter emphasized that the Jewish national identity should be seen in the unity of Jewish writings. Jews were one people characterized by *Einheit* and *Reinheit*. Jewish history and literature, for Schlechter, enforced Jewish national identity. The Jewish *Volk* had *Volksgeschichte* that underscored a pure Jewishness. Schlechter writes regarding the *Einheit* and the *Reinheit* of Jewish identity as expressed in Jewish history and literature: "The selection of Israel, the indestructibility of God's covenant with Israel, the immortality of Israel as a nation, and the final restoration on holy ground, with all the wide-reaching consequences of the conversion of humanity and the establishment

---

[5] Bentwich, *Selected Writings: Solomon Schlechter*, p. 144.

of the kingdom of God on earth – all these are the common ideals and the common ideas that permeate the whole thousand years, including the largest bulk of the Hellenistic portion of it."[6]

For Schlechter, the Jewish *Reich* was an ideal and the central idea undergirding Jewish nationalism. Schlechter like many European nationalists of the nineteenth century emphasized the *Einheit* and the *Reinheit* of the *Reich*. As Schlechter emphasized the unity of Jewish national identity in Jewish history and literature, his examination of Jewish texts followed a Jewish *Reich*-centered interpretation. There was a common character into which all sources expounding over 1,000 years could fit. In fact, in Schlechter's system, it was virtually inconceivable that a Jewish literature could escape the Zionist interpretation.

Solomon Schlechter has had a deep impact on the English speaking world. Schlechter taught at Jews College London, which produced Rabbis for the United Kingdom. Schlechter also taught at British secular institutions, such as the University of London and the University of Cambridge. Eventually, Schlechter gained a dominating influence on world Jewry by becoming the head of the Jewish Theological Seminary.

---

[6] Bentwhich, *Selected Writings: Solomon Schlechter*, pp. 144-145.

Throughout his life Schlechter remained faithful to his nationalistic commitments. Schlechter writes: "Speaking for myself, Zionism was, and still is, the most cherished dream I was worthy of having. It was beautiful to behold the rise of this mighty bulwark against the incessantly assailing forces of assimilation, which became more dangerous, as we have now among us a party permeated by Christian tendencies...."[7] Schlechter's Zionist-tending influence was widely felt in the Jewish world and entered the Gentile world both directly through his publication in English and indirectly through Jewish scholars in various disciplines.

One scholar who heeded Schlechter's call to emphasize a Jewish nationalist interpretation was Geza Vermes. Although trained as a Hebrew scholar who had no intention of researching early Christianity, Vermes wrote perhaps the most controversial book on Jesus of Nazareth in the last century. Entitled, *Jesus the Jew*, Vermes' book emphasized that Jesus must not only be understood in his Jewish context, but that Jesus should be seen as a religious Jew. In positing a Jewish referent, Vermes subscribed to a type of identity that was "pan-Jewish" or "essentially Jewish" in the same

---

[7] Bentwich, *Selected Writings: Solomon Schlechter*, p. 141.

sense that Schlechter and other Zionist scholars of ancient history emphasized.

In other words, Vermes believed that the Jewish identity of the Late Antiquity was more in line with the Jewish characteristics as found in the Old Testament and in contradistinction to the pervasive Hellenistic culture of the time. Specifically, Vermes attacks Martin Hengel for positing a Hellenistic milieu for Jews in Israel. Vermes writes: "In parenthesis, I am of course acquainted with the recent tendencyin New Testament scholarship to seek to efface the difference between Judaism and Hellenism by blurring the frontiers dividing them. But I am firmly convinced of the untenability of Martin Hengel's statement that from 'the middle of the third century BC *all Judaism* must really be designated 'Hellenistic Judaism'...."[8]

As with Schlechter, for Vermes there was an identifiable, distinctive Jewish identity that was homogeneous and continuous for centuries. As such, Vermes privileged a type of *Einheit* and *Reinheit* of Jewish national identity that was perceived and transmitted in the text. Such Zionist interpretation guided Vermes' understanding and interpretation of the Dead Sea Scrolls, his primary area of focus. Vermes writes: "These compositions have not only revived

---

[8] Geza Vermes, *Jesus on the World of Judaism* (London: SCM Press Ltd, 1983), p. 26.

interest in the Jewish background to the New Testament, but in a real, and not journalistic, sense revolutionized it."[9] For Vermes, the revolution is simple; these texts placed Jesus within Judaism. Vermes writes: "In fact, with the discovery and study of the Dead Sea Scrolls and other archaeological treasures, and the corresponding improvements in our understanding of the ideas, doctrines, methods of teaching, language and culture of the Jews in the New Testament times, it is now possible, not simply to place Jesus in relief against this setting, as students of the Jewish background of Christianity prided themselves on doing, but insert him fair and square within first-century Jewish life itself."[10] Geza Vermes thus engages in a Jesus-sat-at-the-feet-of-Moses interpretation of the New Testament and Jesus traditions.

Reclaiming Jesus as a follower of Judaism, Vermes seeks to place him in the context of Galilee and as a charismatic miracle worker. Although Vermes exhibits his more critical side when he argues that Rabbinic literature does not really reflect the reality of Galilee at the time of Jesus,[11] Vermes' homogenizing tendencies are evident when he cites Hanina ben Doza and

---

[9] Vermes, *Jesus and the World of Judaism*, pp. 66-67.
[10] Vermes, *Jesus and the World of Judaism*, p. 2.
[11] Geza Vermes, *Jesus the Jew: A Historian's Reading of the Gospels* (London: Collins, 1973), p. 43.

Honi the Circle Drawer as evidence for Jesus being a Jewish charismatic from Galilee. Besides the problem recognized by Vermes himself of the reliability of Rabbinic sources to describe the Jewish environment in Galilee at the time of Jesus, Vermes' argumentation based on guilt-by-environment-association is problematic. Vermes writes: "It may have been Galilean chauvinism that was responsible for Jesus' apparent antipathy towards Gentiles. For not only did he feel himself sent to Jews alone, he qualified non-Jews, though no doubt with oratorical exaggeration, as 'dogs' and 'swine.'"[12]

In fact, placing Jesus among the non-establishment Galilean Jewish leadership represents Vermes' efforts to reclaim Jesus as a follower of Judaism. To be a leader of Judaism via traditional lines required legal education and association with Jerusalem establishment in the Holy City. The only other way to reach leadership in Judaism was of the charismatic kind and that is where Jesus falls. The emphasis is that Jesus still falls within the Judaism that privileged Zion theology ultimately. So interested is Vermes in placing Jesus within mainstream Judaism (albeit socially outside of the establishment) that he writes:

---

[12] Vermes, *Jesus the Jew: A Historian's Reading of the Gospels*, p. 49.

Jesus became a political suspect in the eyes of the rulers of Jersualem because he was a Galilean. Moreover, if present-day estimates of Jewish historians concerning Galilean lack of education and unorthodoxy are accepted, his same Galilean descent made him a religious suspect also. Should, however, this view of the Galilean character be found tendentious, rabbinic antipathy towards the Galilean and the Pharisees' hostility towards Jesus might justifiably be ascribed, not so much to an aversion to unorthodoxy and lack of education, but simply, as the Israeli scholar, Gedalyahu Alon, insinuates, to a sentiment of superiority on the part of the intellectual *élite* of the metropolis towards unsophisticated provincials.[13]

For Vermes, Jesus was a follower of Judaism who happened to be in the wrong side of the barricade. Vermes describes the stigma of being a Galilean Jew this way: "In

---

[13] Vermes, *Jesus the Jew: A Historian's Reading of the Gospels*, p. 57.

Jerusalem, and in Judaean circles, they had also the reputation of being an unsophisticated people. In rabbinic parlance, a Galilean is usually referred to as *Galili Shoteh*, stupid Galilean. He is represented as a typical 'peasant,' a boor, a 'am ha-arez, a religiously uneducated person."[14] Even though there was friction between Galilean Jews and the Jerusalem establishment, Vermes stresses the fundamental *Einheit* of Jews as a *Volk*. Jesus fell within Jewish national identity and not outside it. And like a good Zionist, Vermes assumes Jewish religious identity integrated with Jewish national identity. Vermes, like Schlechter, is a product of the nineteenth century European nationalism.

While stressing the *Einheit* of Jewishness, Vermes is quick to dismiss ties between Jesus and Christianity. Vermes writes: "Turning now to Christian religion and religiousness as distinct from the religiousness and religion of Jesus, I am aware that for the vast majority of Christians – and many Jews for that matter – the very statement that Jesus and Christianity are to be differentiated from one another will come as a shock, a total surprise."[15] For Vermes, Jesus was a follower of Judaism and not a founder of Christianity. In *Jesus in His*

---

[14] Geza Vermes, *Jesus in His Jewish Context* (London: SCM Press, 2003), pp. 4-5.

[15] Vermes, *Jesus and the World of Judaism*, p. 54.

*Jewish Context*, published in 2003, Vermes writes: "'Jesus the Jew – which is also the title of a book I have written – is an emotionally charged synonym for the Jesus of history as opposed to the divine Christ of the Christian faith that simply re-states the obvious fact, still hard for many Christians and even some Jews to accept, that Jesus was a Jew and not a Christian. It implies a renewed quest for the historical figure reputed to be the founder of Christianity."[16] Vermes argued that Christian elements were later imputing of Gentile focused Christianity and not attributable to Jesus. In essence, Vermes subscribes to a type of "Catholic Israel" in which Jesus participated. Certainly, a Jewish nationalistic interpretation influenced Vermes' reading into the Jewishness of Jesus and his aggressive efforts to cut Jesus out of his Christian place.

Vermes credits the Holocaust as allowing him to practice such a Jewish nationalist reading of the New Testament and Jesus tradition. Vermes writes: "The recent developments in our domain are attributable to two main causes. The first is the impact on the Christian world of the horror of the Holocaust . .... In the shadow of the chimneys of the death-camps, anti-Judaism, even academic anti-Judaism has become no only unfashionable but obscene.

---

[16] Vermes, *Jesus in His Jewish Context*, p. 1.

For the moment at least, it has largely disappeared, and we have now a more open, positive and constructive approach by New Testament scholars towards post-biblical Judaism."[17] In essence, two European nationalists propelled New Testament interpretation in the direction that Vermes desired.

I would argue that a nationalist interpretation of this kind does disservice to the study of the ancient world. Not only are there problems from critical and methodological vantage points, such a nationalist interpretation skews understanding of historical reality from the start. This paper focused on the critique of a nationalist interpretation of the New Testament and was limited to that critique due to time constraints. The positive side of the critique is my emphasis that a more localized, in-group research will be more constructive to understanding the historical reality. From a methodological standpoint, I would refer to my paper delivered at the Society of Biblical Literature Annual Meeting in Atlanta, Georgia, in 2003, as a starting point for the shift in methodology. And I hope to publish the proceedings from that conference and this paper also with the hope of bringing the study of first-century Israel to a more accurate historical understanding.

---

[17] Vermes, *Jesus and the World of Judaism*, p. 66.

## About the Author

Heerak Christian Kim received his B.A. *cum laude* in history with a minor in classical studies from the University of Pennsylvania in Philadelphia. Kim received his M.A. in history in 1991 at the University of California, Los Angeles (UCLA) in the context of the Ph.D. program in the History Department. Kim pursued his theological training part-time while being a full-time student at UCLA and obtained his MA in Theology from Fuller Seminary in Pasadena.

Kim has conducted doctoral level research at the Hebrew University of Jerusalem, Harvard University, Brown University, and the University of Heidelberg in Germany. Currently, Kim is a Ph.D. candidate in Hebrew, Jewish, and Early Christian Studies at the University of Cambridge in the United Kingdom and resident at Jesus College, Cambridge.

Kim has received many prestigious fellowships and scholarships during the course of his research, such as the Lady Davis Fellowship and the Raoul Wallenberg

Scholarship. Kim has taught undergraduate students at UCLA and Brown University. In Cambridge, Two separate committees (the New Testament Committee and the Old Testament Committee) have appointed him as a supervisor of undergraduate students at the University of Cambridge to teach courses in Hebrew, Jewish, and Early Christian Studies.

Currently, Heerak Christian Kim is particularly interested in methodological questions regarding the study of Biblical texts and ancient history. His ongoing research projects also include examining Jewish Law in the context of legal history and in comparison to modern legal systems, an interest sparked while studying the Talmud with Professor Isaiah Gafni when he was a visiting professor at Harvard University in 1999.

www.ingramcontent.com/pod-product-compliance
Lightning Source LLC
Chambersburg PA
CBHW031148160426
43193CB00008B/294